KILBURN AND WEST HAMPSTEAD PAST

Acknowledgements

We would like to thank Ian Johnston, of Brent Local History Archive; Richard Knight, Malcolm Holmes, Aidan Flood and Lesley Marshall of Camden Local Studies and Archives Centre, for all their help. Thanks are also due to James James Crook and Mr and Mrs Marley for allowing us to publish copies of their photographs.

The Illustrations

Illustrations have been reproduced with the kind permission of the following:

Anon: *39*

The London Borough of Brent: *2, 9, 11, 15, 19, 20, 21, 22, 23, 24, 26, 31, 62, 63, 76, 85, 133*

The London Borough of Camden: *4, 6, 7, 8, 12, 14, 28, 29, 32, 34, 35, 36, 43, 47, 50, 51, 56, 57, 59, 60, 89, 92, 95, 106, 108, 112, 116, 117, 118, 119, 126, 129, 130, 131, 135, 136 and the jacket*

Roger Cline: *1*

Marianne Colloms: *10, 16, 17, 18, 30, 38, 42, 44, 45, 46, 52, 53, 54, 55, 58, 61, 65, 66, 68, 71, 73, 74, 75, 77, 78, 79, 80, 81, 82, 83, 84, 86, 90, 91, 93, 94, 96, 97, 99, 100, 101, 102, 103, 104, 105, 113, 114, 115, 120, 121, 123, 125, 127, 128, 132*

James James Crook: *27, 48, 49, 64, 67, 87, 107, 134*

John Lewis Partnership: *139*

Mr and Mrs Marley: *40, 41*

All others were supplied by Historical Publications.

First published 1999
by Historical Publications Ltd
32 Ellington Street, London N7 8PL
(Tel: 020-7607 1628)

ISBN 0 948667 59 1
British Library Cataloguing-in-Data
A catalogue record for this book is available from the British Library

Typeset in Palatino by Historical Publications
Reproduction by G & J Graphics, London EC2
Printed in Zaragoza, Spain by Edelvives

KILBURN AND WEST HAMPSTEAD PAST

Dick Weindling
Marianne Colloms

HISTORICAL PUBLICATIONS

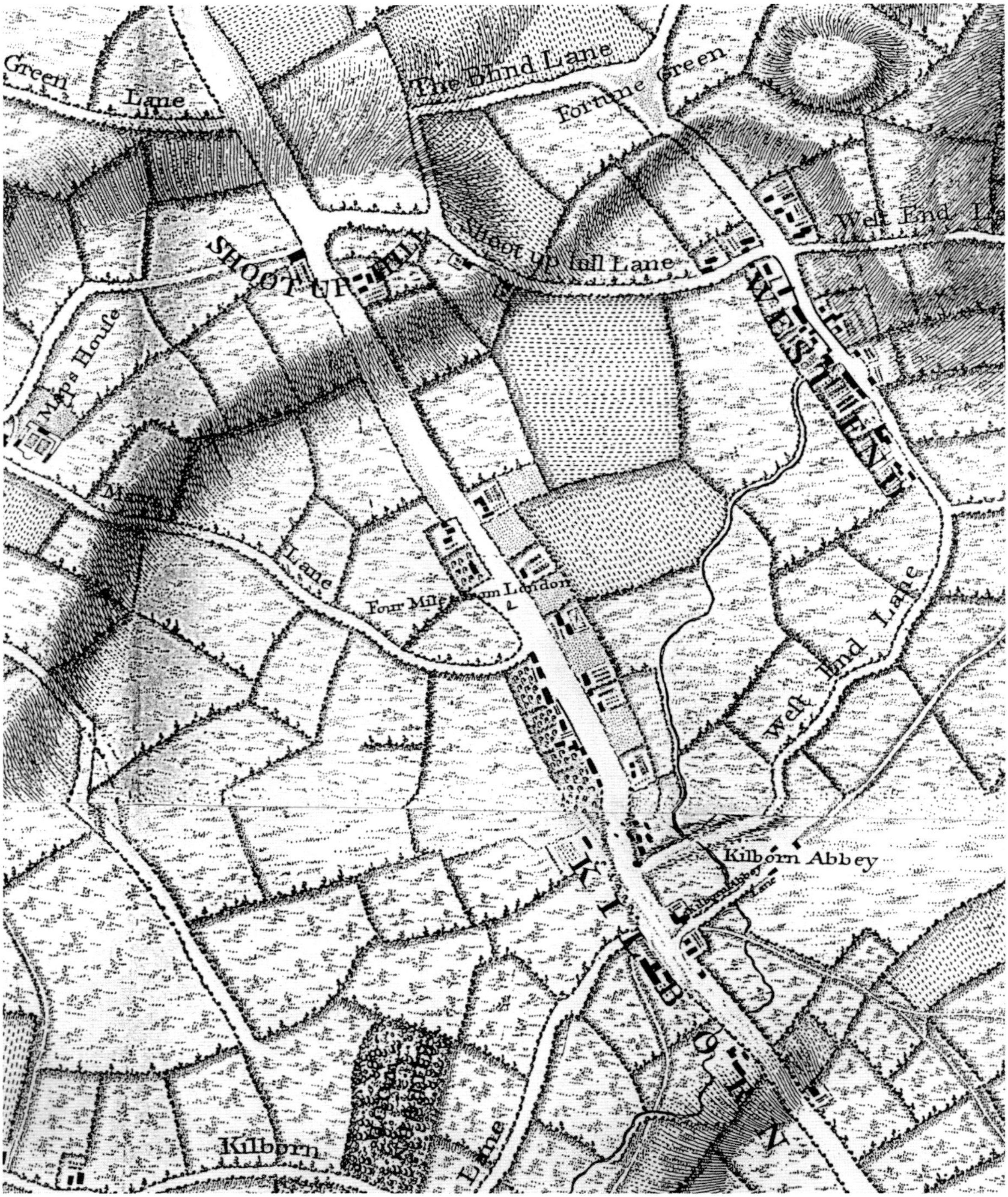

1. *John Rocque's map of the environs of London, c.1745, showing the villages of Kilburn and West End.*

Contents

2. *Kilburn Priory buildings in use as a farm (date unknown).*

Early Days

ON THE ROMAN ROAD

The village of Kilburn grew up on both sides of the road leading from London to St Albans, one of the earliest roads built by the Romans after they landed on the Kent coast in AD 43. Watling Street, as it was later called, ran from the Roman fort in Richborough, Kent to London and then through St Albans to Chester. The name 'Watling Street' is mentioned in the Treaty of Wedmore (AD 878) between King Alfred and the Danes, when the latter agreed to leave Wessex and settle on the northern side of Watling Street, leaving the southern side for the Saxons. The straight road, built by the Romans to move their troops quickly, shows clearly on early maps when it was called the London Way (1599) and later the Edgware Road. In 1923 workmen digging in Kilburn found flint blocks from the Roman road at a depth of about six feet. The road marked the boundary between Willesden on one side and Hampstead on the other – today's London boroughs of Brent and Camden.

An early reference to Kilburn occurs in 1455. Richard, Duke of York, together with other nobles had taken up arms and marched south. They wrote from Ware, in Hertfordshire to Archbishop Bourchier declaring that they were as ready as anyone to defend King Henry VI. Bourchier sent word to that effect by a special messenger to the King who was on his way to Leicester. However, when the messenger reached the army at Kilburn, the message was read by Lord Somerset but not delivered to the King. A second letter was also withheld from Henry, so that when he came to St Albans he saw Richard's army outside the town as hostile. The ensuing battle, in which Somerset was killed and the King himself wounded, was the beginning of the War of the Roses.

The name of Kilburn is usually thought to be derived from the stream that rose in Hampstead and flowed down the hill through West End to Kilburn. It ran parallel to the High Road along what is today's Kingsgate Road before passing under the main road at Kilburn Bridge. The stream was culverted to form part of the Ranelagh sewer in the 1860s. In ancient documents Kilburn is spelt in various ways such as Kyllbourne, Kelebourne, Kulleburne. Its meaning has been the cause of much debate but is probably derived from the Anglo-Saxon *Kyle* (cold) and Bourne (water). Another variation of the name was Kilnbourn, which possibly indicates a derivation from tile-making in the area.

KILBURN PRIORY

Our knowledge of early Kilburn centres on the Priory which was situated near the intersection of today's Belsize Road, Kilburn Vale and the railway. At the beginning of the 12th Century a hermit called Godwin built himself a small cell or hermitage at 'Cuneburn' next to the stream. When in 1134 this was made over to Westminster Abbey, three nuns or 'handmaidens of Christ', Emma, Gunhilda and Christina, established a Benedictine nunnery on the site. Possibly, they were former maids of honour to Queen Matilda, the wife of Henry I. The conditions for this transfer were that Godwin would be the Warden until he died, and a Chaplain would be appointed to oversee the nuns. The Bishop of London disputed Westminster's jurisdiction over the convent, but this was resolved in Westminster's favour in 1231.

The church erected at the Priory was dedicated to St John the Baptist. The property seems to have been added to from time to time in return for prayers for the souls of the brethren who had once belonged to Westminster. Soon after its establishment Abbot Herbert gave the nuns an estate called Gara, in the Manor of Knightsbridge, at Kensington Gore, and they also received gifts of wine and food. The Priory held land in Kent, Southwark, Tottenham and Hendon. The manor farm of Wembley, in the parish of Harrow, also appears to have belonged to it.

However, in 1352 the Priory was found to be in great distress by the Bishop of London and was exempted from taxes. In 1382, the Priory building was found to be much decayed and the nuns pleaded debt, due to their situation near a busy highway, and the burden of affording hospitality to people, both rich and poor, who continually passed along the road. Large numbers of people made a pilgrimage to St Albans and one of the duties of the nuns was to give

3. The seal of Kilburn Priory. In 1290 it depicted a lamb and flag with the moon and a star, while in 1536 it portrayed (as here) John the Baptist in a camel-haired garment.

4. Today, the only remaining relic of the Priory is the small brass tablet that is now in St Mary's Church, Priory Road. This was unearthed in 1878 and was thought to depict the prioress Emma de Sancto Omero.

5. The remains of Kilburn Priory, c.1750.

a night's lodging to travellers. It was an important service because after ascending Shoot Up Hill the road to St Albans went through dense oak forests that provided excellent cover for robbers. The pilgrims waited at the foot of the hill to form companies for protection.

To assist the nuns, an acre of land and the church at Cudham in Kent was appropriated to Kilburn Priory by the Bishop of Rochester, and other small bequests were made by individuals throughout the 14th and 15th centuries. Despite these, and the rentals from the grants of land, the convent never became wealthy.

Only seven of the prioresses of Kilburn can be traced. The earliest to be identified is Joan, prioress in 1255 and the next who can be traced is Cecilia, who received payments in 1290. Alice de Pomesbourne, prioress of Kilburn, held a lease on a tenement in Bow Lane in 1339, and about 1400 the name of Emma de Sancto Omero (*see ill. 4*) appears on a lease. Matilda Reynold is named as prioress in 1465 for an annual payment to Westminster Abbey and Margery is identified from a deed. The last named prioress at Kilburn, at the time of the dissolution of the monasteries, is Anne Browne.

Remarkably, in spite of all its difficulties, the Priory continued its daily support for travellers for 400 years until 1536 when it was dissolved, classified as a lesser monastery (under £200 value). At this time the 'Nonnerie of Kilnborne' was valued at £74. 7s 11d, and included the Priory Farm, outbuildings and land. (Other authorities give values of £86 or £121.)

Our best information about the Priory comes from an inventory dated 11 May 1536, the year of dissolution, which details the rooms and furniture for the church, house, brewhouse and bakehouse. The description of the fixtures and fittings shows that the Priory was not wealthy. The more valuable items – wall hangings, candlesticks, two silver chalices and goblets – are itemised, and the Priory also possessed, 'one horse of the coller of blacke', valued at 5s.

The dissolution marked the end of the Priory as an ecclesiastical site and it then passed through a complex line of ownership. Henry VIII did not keep the property long and he exchanged it with the Order of the Knights of St John of Jerusalem for their manor in Paris Garden, Southwark, which was much more valuable. But four years later, when the larger monasteries and the Knights of St John were dissolved, Kilburn came back to the Crown. The estate was then sold into lay ownership. In the 18th century it was owned by the Liddells who sold the greater part (Shoot Up Hill, Kilburn Woods and the family's farm) to the Powell Cottons and disposed of the remainder to Richard Marsh (Abbey Farm). The Priory buildings at that time were occupied as a dwelling house.

Over time the buildings fell into disuse and stones were taken as building material for other houses. A sketch map of the Priory grounds dated 1790 (now in the British Library), notes that the last of the remaining Priory buildings was pulled down 'some months ago'. This important document shows the location of the Priory in relation to the streams from Child's Hill and Hampstead. Park, writing in 1814, says that all the remains of the Priory are long since destroyed. 'Although the site is still distinguishable by a rising bank in a field adjoining the Wells, and till of late there was a barn built on the ruined walls'. He includes an engraving from 1722 which only shows a small building, probably a domestic outbuilding, which is all that remained at the time.

When the railway was cut through in the autumn of 1852, some pottery, a few coins and a bronze vessel, all medieval, were found at the Priory site and these were put on display at the Archaeological Institute.

The Middlesex Sessions records for 2 September 1613 provide an example of how the Priory buildings were looted over time. John Earle of Kilburn, a labourer, was committed for stealing two iron chains worth 5 shillings, a hatchet worth 12 pence, two double hooks worth 12 pence, and three iron pins worth 4 pence. Earle confessed, and was found guilty and sentenced to be whipped and led to gaol.

In 1659 there is an indictment against Thomas Tramplett, prisoner at Newgate, who was accused of having 'feloniously taken out of an Abbey, by name Kilbourne Abbey, 16 iron casements and frames for casements, a barre of iron and other pieces of iron'.

THE BLEEDING STONE OF KILBURN

In 1817 William Atkinson, of Grove End, St John's Wood, wrote a short pamphlet entitled, *The Bleeding Stone of Kilburn* in which he said that a stone was still to be seen at a place called 'Red Barn', near St John's Wood, which was 'connected with the records of Kilburn Priory by a wild and singular legend of superstition'. 'This stone is reported to have been brought from the shores of Whitby in Yorkshire, by order of Stephen de Merton, for the purpose of erecting a shrine'. Atkinson then describes the large stone which had a dark reddish stain on one side, and he recounted a medieval story which told of the murder of Sir Gervase de Merton by his brother Stephen for the love of Gervase's wife. The bloody deed took place on the shores of Whitby and stained the stone. Stephen returned to Kilburn and unable to subdue the Lady, he threw her into a dungeon where she died. Later, racked with guilt, he had the remains of his brother exhumed from Whitby and buried with his wife in Kilburn, where he erected a costly shrine from stones brought from Whitby, including the Bleeding Stone on which his brother had died. When Stephen 'saw the bloody mark flow afresh and heard a groan' he fled and confessed to Gilbert, Bishop of London. He then left all his lands and wealth to Kilburn Priory and became a monk. Atkinson attaches what he calls, 'an old Ballad upon the subject, but evidently of a much later date, [that] testifies the existence of the legend'. This is a poem about the story in 29 verses.

William Atkinson was an architect who built a number of country houses, including Sir Walter Scott's 'Abbotsford'. He invented Atkinson's Cement, the raw materials of which were shipped to his wharf in Westminster from Whitby. About 1817 he moved to a house in Grove End, St John's Wood, near Lord's Cricket Ground, where he lived until about 1830. The house was close to Sir Edwin Landseer's house, which had been built in 1824 on the site of a property previously called Punkers Barn, or Red Barn, at the crossroads of what are now St John's Wood Road and Grove End Road.

The *Athenaeum* journal (date unknown) published a poem by Sir Walter Scott entitled, *The Muckle Stain or the Bleeding Stone of Kilburn Priory*. This is a slightly shorter version of the poem quoted by Atkinson in 1817, with some minor differences. What is extremely revealing is the introductory note from the unnamed correspondent attached to the poem:

> My late father was a friend of Scott's, and helped him in the decoration and finishings of Abbotsford. Scott would often dine with my father when in London, and was greatly interested in the garden. In one corner there was some rockwork, in which were inserted some fragments of stone ornaments from the ruins of Kilburn Priory: and crowning all, was

a large irregularly shaped stone, having a deep red stain, no doubt of ferruginous origin. This stone was sent to my father by Lord Mulgrave in one of his cement vessels, my father having been struck with its appearance on the shore at Whitby: and from these simple really unconnected facts, Scott made out the following story, in verses, which might be regarded as a kind of friendly offering in return for the services rendered.

What can we conclude from all this? We have established a link between William Atkinson, Sir Walter Scott, Lord Mulgrave at Whitby, and Kilburn Priory. It seems that Atkinson, a keen geologist, took parts of the Priory ruins for the garden of his new house in Grove End about 1817. He also installed a large stone with a red stain shipped to him from Whitby by Lord Mulgrave. Atkinson showed these stones to Sir Walter Scott who wrote the poem about Stephen and Gervase de Merton. After Scott's death in 1832 and Atkinson's death in 1839, the poem was sent for publication in the *Athenaeum* by one of his sons (William or Henry George Atkinson). There is no trace of Stephen and Gervase de Merton (or Mertoun, Morton, Mortoune, as it appears in the various versions of the story) in any medieval references. Thus we can only conclude that Scott and Atkinson created the story and that it has no historical foundation at all. It would be fascinating to know if the stone has survived in the gardens of one of the modern houses near Grove End Road.

KILBURN BRIDGE

The old Kelebourne stream rose in the heights of Hampstead and flowed down through West Hampstead to a point near Brondesbury Station. Here it turned south and ran parallel to the Kilburn High Road, passing under a small bridge on West End Lane, to the junction of Belsize Road and Kilburn Vale. Here it formed a small lake in the pleasure grounds of Kilburn Wells. The stream crossed the Edgware Road under Kilburn Bridge. It then joined the Westbourne near today's Shirland Road, and then flowed to the Serpentine and eventually reached the Thames near Chelsea Bridge.

Kilburn Bridge was probably built for Kilburn Priory in the mid-13th Century. In 1826 Kilbourne Bridge was described as 'being made of brick and stone with one arch; it is 37 feet wide'. The waterway beneath was 7 feet wide and 6 feet high. The middle part of the bridge was the original stone structure with a Gothic arch, which had been widened with brick on either side. At this time repairs for the southern side of the road were the responsibility of the St Marylebone turnpike trust, while the northern side of the bridge was that of the Kilburn Road trust.

KILBURN WELLS

In the 18th century Kilburn gained a reputation for the medicinal properties of a well that was almost as celebrated as Hampstead Wells. A spring known as Kilburn Wells was situated to the rear of the Bell Tavern, in Abbey Fields, near the site of the old Kilburn Priory. The Gardens were enlarged and improved by the proprietor as shown by the following advertisement in the *Public Advertiser* of 17 July 1773.

'Kilburn Wells, near Paddington. The waters now are in the utmost perfection: the gardens enlarged and greatly improved; the house and offices re-painted and beautiful in the most elegant manner. The whole is now open for the reception of the public, the great room being particularly adapted to the use and amusement of the politest companies. Fit either for music, dancing or entertainments. This happy spot is equally celebrated for its rural situation, extensive prospects, and the acknowledged efficacy of its waters; it is most delightfully situated near the site of the once famous Abbey of Kilburn, on the Edgware Road, at an easy distance, being but a morning's walk, from the metropolis, two miles from Oxford Street; the foot-way from the Mary-bone across the fields is still nearer. A plentiful larder is always provided, together with the best of wines and other liquors. Breakfasting and hot loaves.'

In 1801 Dr John Bliss carried out a series of experiments and analysed the water from both Kilburn and Hampstead wells. Writing about Kilburn he said:

'The spring rises about twelve feet below the surface and is enclosed in a large brick reservoir, which bears the date of 1714 on the key stone of the arch over the door. The water collected in the well, is usually of the depth of five or six feet, but in a dry Summer it is from three to four, at which time its effect as a purgative is increased. .... When taken fresh from the well a few inches under the surface it is tolerably clear, but not of a crystal transparency: at first it is insipid, but leaves an evident saline taste on the tongue. At rest, and even on slight agitation, no smell is produced but on stirring the water forcibly from the bottom of the reservoir, it becomes turbid from impurities which have been collected in it, and a considerable odour is emitted like that from the scouring of a foul gun barrel.'

Bliss said that when from one to three pints were taken at very short intervals the purgative operation was slow and gentle. He recommended it for indigestion and various other problems. The use of the water for curative purposes appears to have ceased in the early part of the 19th century. But the Old Bell, or Kilburn Wells enjoyed continuing popularity as a tea garden and tavern.

In 1829, a newspaper reported a competition:

'On Friday last a grand pigeon match, for 50 sovereigns, took place at Mr Morley's Bell Tavern, Kilburn - eleven picked shots of Hampstead against eleven picked shots of Kilburn. It commenced at four o'clock. Hampstead fired at six dozen birds, out of which they killed five dozen and two, missing only ten birds. Kilburn followed, and out of their six dozen killed five dozen and seven, winning by five birds. We have scarcely seen better firing, and the ground is excellently adapted for this sport. The parties afterwards sat down to an excellent supper, provided by the worthy host.' (1829)

It is thought that the tea gardens described by Dickens and pictured by Cruikshank in *Sketches by Boz* could be those at Kilburn.

In 1837 the line of the London & Birmingham Railway (later the London & North Western) was cut through the gardens, after which the part just behind the pub was used as a tea garden and another part which contained the well was made into a kitchen garden, but to get to the well from the house the railway bridge had to be crossed. Then in 1863 the Old Bell itself was pulled down and the present public house was erected on the spot. The well, which stood immediately behind the Bank at the corner of Belsize Road, was demolished and built over. A stone plaque on the building that is now occupied by Holland and Barrett, the health food shop, points out that the well was there.

KILBURN MILL

At the top of Shoot Up Hill on the Willesden side was a windmill for grinding corn, probably built by William Bonington in 1798. From 1799 to 1801 a Mr Jenkins was rated, and then Isaac Ennos owned it from 1802 to 1828. In addition, Ennos owned two fields on the Hampstead side, off Mill Lane, as well as some tenements near the Old Black Lion in West End Lane. In 1829 the mill passed to his son-in-law, William Hale.

6. A drawing of c.1750, thought to be the Long Room at Kilburn, c.1750.

7. In 1837, the tracks of the London & Birmingham Railway (later the LNWR) crossed the fields of Abbey Farm and went under the Kilburn High Road, cutting the Bell public house off from the old Well. In compensation, the line provided a new if relatively infrequent source of amusement for visitors to the tea gardens – train spotting!

8. Kilburn Mill. This type was known as a smock mill, as the sloping shape was supposed to resemble the smock costume of an agricultural labourer.

9. The steam flour mill at Shoot Up Hill in 1890. Surprisingly, the burnt remains of the older Kilburn windmill outlasted its steam successor, and an old lady writing in 1953 recalled how she and her friends had swung on the sails as children. It finally collapsed in 1903.

Business thrived and by 1851 Hale employed five men. In 1859 he built a new steam mill alongside the old structure.

Charles Hale, his son, was the owner when the mill was burnt down. It has been a matter for debate as to when this happened, but according to Fire Brigade reports, it was on 23 December 1863. *The Times* records that the weather was very bad, with gales causing considerable damage around the country. Local tradition has it that the gale blew the sails around so fast that the friction caused the fire and the windmill burnt like a giant Catherine wheel. But the fire also spread to the house and its glare attracted thousands of people some of whom helped to carry out furniture. It has even been claimed that the Prince of Wales, who had an interest in fire brigades, watched the fire, but this cannot be substantiated. The nearest fire engine was called from Paddington at 5pm but arrived too late to help. The old mill, the new mill of four floors, a large shed, the timber and a yard were burned down, the upper floor of the house was burnt out and the roof was off. The rest of the house and contents were severely damaged by fire, water and removal. As a result of the accident Willesden Vestry agreed to establish the Kilburn Volunteer Fire Brigade soon afterwards.

Charles Hale left the old windmill derelict and continued to use the steam mill to grind corn, but by 1871 he had sold out to the Bates Brothers – it appears in the local directories as 'Kilburn Flour Mills', operated by R. and A. Bates. It ceased operation in 1891 and was pulled down in 1898, some forty years after it was built.

An amusing incident concerning the old windmill was reported in 1839 under the heading of 'A Modern Quixote'.

> 'At Marylebone an eccentric-looking being, who gave his name as Edward Walden, was charged with the following Quixotic attack on a windmill, erected near Kilburn. He primed and loaded a fowling-piece with which he was furnished and marched gallantly up the hill on which the windmill was situated, and without the least parlay placed the gun to his shoulder and fired in the direction of the sails. Police constable 206D, who observed the prisoner, stepped forward and took him into custody. The knight of woeful countenance assured the magistrate that he owned the windmill no ill-will or spite: in proof of which

10. The road to Hampstead. This shows the bridge over the Kilbourne on West End Lane, as seen from the Kilburn High Road.

he averred before marching to the attack he had taken especial care to withdraw the charge of shot from the piece, and he hoped the owner of the mill would be equally ready to withdraw the present serious charge against him. The magistrates seemed to be of opinion that a windmill which had stood so many breezes was not in much danger of being blown up by the fowling-piece of a cockney Quixote. They therefore dismissed the Don on the payment of five shillings.'

KILBURN LIFE

A road map of 1749 by Messeder shows very few large houses along the High Road. Travelling from London on the Edgware Road the beginning of Kilburn was marked by the bridge over the Kilborne stream. About a 100 yards further was the tollgate and then on opposite sides of the road were the Red Lion and the Kilburn Manor House. Next came The Bell with its purging wells, while on the Willesden side was the pound for stray animals. The only other large houses on the Willesden side were Kilburn House and then along Mapes Lane (now Willesden Lane) were Brands and Mapes Houses. Elm Row was shown near the fourth mile stone (from London), and the last house was at the top of Shoot Up Hill.

Some idea of life in Kilburn at the beginning of the 19th Century is given by newspaper reports of a bare-knuckle fight and the more upper-class foot race.

(1804)
'A fight took place in Tare Field, at Kilburn, between Handy, a gentleman's coachman, and Anstey, a higgler (a peddler). Each had staked ten guineas last June to fight for the sum in the next six months. The odds were in favour of the coachman, who is known in the old pugilistic schools by the appellation, 'Young Ben'. In the 54th round Handy was hit hard in the stomach and was unable to rise. This decided the contest after an hour and a half.'

(1806)
'A foot race for fifty guineas was run yesterday morning at Pine Apple Place, on the Kilburn Road, between a Capt. of an Irish regiment of infantry, and Mr Barton, an attorney. The distance was 150 yards, and the odds at starting were in favour of Mr Barton. The Captain had the start, and kept the advantage until 90 yards had been run, when Mr B. who had kept close in with his opponent, passed him, and won the race easy, leaving the Captain about eight yards in the rear.'

An item from 1815 illustrated the danger of a dog bite and told how John Kiff, a gardener at Kilburn Wells, had been bitten on the leg. But despite immediate medical attendance by dressing the wounds and taking doses of a remedy, he died of hydrophobia (rabies) six weeks later, leaving a widow with two children.

HIGHWAY CRIME

Crime was probably no worse in the Kilburn area than in any other of the small villages around London. The Middlesex Sessions of 29 August 1613, record a case in which Edward Sheppard of Kilburn, a baker, was charged for 'assault and battery on Hugh Woode at the same'. However, Sheppard had gone on the run and was still 'at large'.

Horse-stealing is recorded in 1772:

'A set of villains have lately made it their practice to steal horses from the farmers etc. round Paddington, Kilburn and Wilsden and sell them to a man at the skirts of the town who used to kill them in the night, for the sake of their skins, flesh and bones, the latter of which he boiled in cauldrons, a great number of fine horse from £10 to £30 value have been destroyed. One of the gang has turned evidence, and impeached several of his companions.'

But inevitably, at the end of the 18th century, Kilburn's position on a main highway led to local robberies, several of them violent, from travellers. In 1774 it was reported that:

'Two gentlemen returning from a shooting party in Hertfordshire had heard that footpads had previously robbed the very post-chaise they were in. They kept their guns ready. Between Kilburn and Paddington three fellows on foot, whose appearance created suspicion, advanced in the road, then separated to the right and left, and on a sudden one of them seized the bridal of the horse on which the boy rode, while the other two came to each door with pistols in their hands. The gentleman who was outside, immediately lodged the contents of his piece in the breast of one of the gang, who staggered a few paces and fell, in all probability dangerously wounded: on that another of the villains discharged his pistol, the ball of which damaged a trunk that was fastened in front of the carriage. The gentleman who had fired successfully, that instant quitted his situation, and with the butt end of his gun made a blow at the fellow who stood at the horses, with such violence that the stocke broke, and would have been fatal, had it not been pared off by a pistol which was afterwards snapt, though happily without effect. The gentleman in the chaise, alarmed at the danger his friend was in, jumped out to assist him, which prevented the villains from returning to the charge, and defeated their design.'

A curious encounter is reported in 1806:

'On Friday night, about nine o'clock a post-chaise returning from London to Edgware, near Kilburn Wells, was stopped by a footpad. The driver was in the chaise, with two men, and on finding the chaise stopped, he looked out of the window to see the villain who demanded their money or their lives. One of the men was asleep, and the noise awoke him: he told the robber he would not give his money, for he might as well go home without his brains as without his money. The driver told the robber his was only a return chaise, and he did not think his passengers had any property about them. The robber then shook hands with them all, and bid them good night. When the man who had been asleep had hold of the robber's hand, he told him he had a great mind not to let go.'

DUELLING

Although duelling was frowned upon by the authorities (it was made illegal in 1819), numerous affairs of honour were fought and were well publicised. They were particularly prevalent among young military men. A number took place in Kilburn and near the Wells. On 2 July 1792 Lord Lauderdale and General Arnold met to end a long misunderstanding. Charles James Fox was Lauderdale's second and Lord Hawke the General's. The press reported that Lauderdale received his antagonist's fire unhurt, but he declined to return the shot. Observing that he had not come there to shoot the General, he could not however retract the words he had used; therefore if General Arnold was not satisfied, he might fire till he was. On consulting the seconds, the affair was considered to be ended. In fact Lord Lauderdale had, only a few days before, duelled with the Duke of Richmond on the same spot.

Again, in 1808:

'An affair of honour took place on Saturday morning, in the fields at the back of the Cock public house, at Kilburn, between Mr S-, a gentleman who was recently on the Staff of the Guards, and W—n, Esq. a merchant. The parties disagreed at the opera Concert, and they had

11. An early photograph of the Victoria Riflemen. James Crook is shown standing third from the left (see also p.77).

12. *The Victoria Rifle Corps at Kilburn. Their grounds were near today's Victoria Road.*

met to fight on Friday morning, but the combat was deferred from a supposed interruption. The combatants had three fires each, and, in the last fire, Mr S- was severely wounded in the cheek, the ball having taken a slanting course, and his adversary was hit dangerously in the left arm. Captain P- and a Mr Rogers were seconds.'

THE VICTORIA RIFLES

The Cumberland Sharpshooters were founded in 1792 as a volunteer unit. In 1814 they became a civilian rifle club based at Covent Garden, but met for drill and practice at Wormwood Scrubs and Kensal Green. The name was changed in 1835 to the Royal Victoria Rifle Club and, following a disagreement with the landlord of the Kensal Green ground, they leased 14 acres on the Willesden side of Kilburn High Road in 1849. The Club became a military unit in 1853, known as the Victoria Rifles. In 1859 it was renamed the 1st Middlesex Rifle Volunteers and they left Kilburn in 1867 when Victoria Road was built across the range, moving to the Roundwood Estate. Their name was remembered by the pub 'The Rifle Volunteer' which is now 'The Bridge'.

WEST END

The sunken roadway of West End Lane entered the village of West End under a canopy of tall elm trees, so well established they met overhead in places. The raised footpath was edged by iron posts supporting a metal chain fence. It was so quiet that locals reported hearing the guns of Waterloo and much later, the chimes of Big Ben. The Lane was bordered by large houses and a number of cottages. A few more cottages round the corner in Mill Lane, including the village smithy and the home of the letter carrier who took the village post up the hill to Hampstead, completed the houses of the less well-off inhabitants. Some worked for their wealthier neighbours as domestic servants and gardeners, or took in laundry. But there was certainly a good deal of poverty. West End clung to its village-like atmosphere well into the 1890s, due in no small part to the continuing existence of several of these large houses and extensive grounds right in the heart of the community.

13. Pen and ink drawing by Fancourt, c.1840, probably looking down Fortune Green Road towards the village of West End.

14. Pen and ink drawing by Fancourt, showing the view from the Cock and Hoop in West End Lane. The buildings on the left were part of the West End House estate. Those on the right were Providence Place on West End Lane.

Country Life and the Gentry

The neighbourhoods of West End and Kilburn were very different. Kilburn could hardly be called a traditional village, as it had no central heart. Houses and cottages straggled in a broken line along the Edgware Road, but there were also a number of inns catering to long-distance coach services along the High Road. West End had no such service, saw little passing traffic and could claim to be a real village, with a farm and a pond on its green. Even after Finchley Road was built in 1829 West End remained relatively isolated, on a route that for many years went nowhere other than Hampstead village. The outward spread of London was only just beginning, when in 1829 John Pocock, a young boy who lived in one of the new houses built by his father on Maida Vale, recorded a stag hunt in his diary.

> 'A beautiful stag, hunted by His Majesty's hounds and about 60 riders of distinction passed our schoolroom windows. He made off for Kilburn and was turned close to our house. The whole neighbourhood presented a very lively appearance from the number of huntsmen in their scarlet coats, the stag set off in the direction of Paddington and coming to the Grand Union Canal swam across towards the church, it so happened the door was open and he bounded in and was caught inside the church! The poor creature who was a victim to this inhuman sport must have given chase at least 35 miles as he was started at Hounslow and had made a long circuitous route.'

Local estates included Abbey Farm which lay south of West End Lane. It included the site of

15. Old Kilburn Manor House (Bounds), which occupied a site between today's Oxford and Cambridge Roads. This is the only known picture of the building in existence and shows the house hidden behind trees and boarded up for sale.

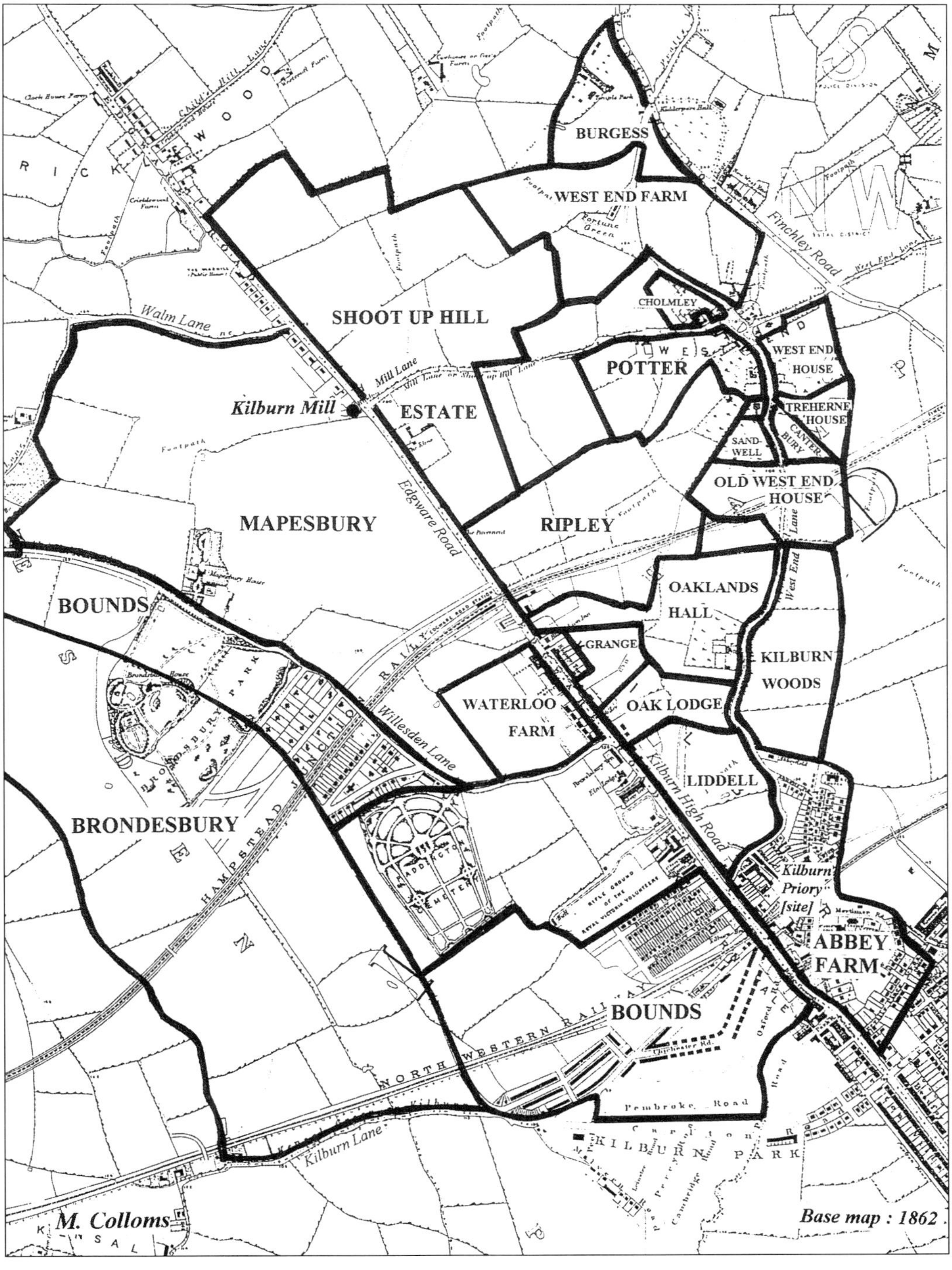

16. *A map, compiled by Marianne Colloms, showing estate boundaries in the Kilburn and West End areas.*

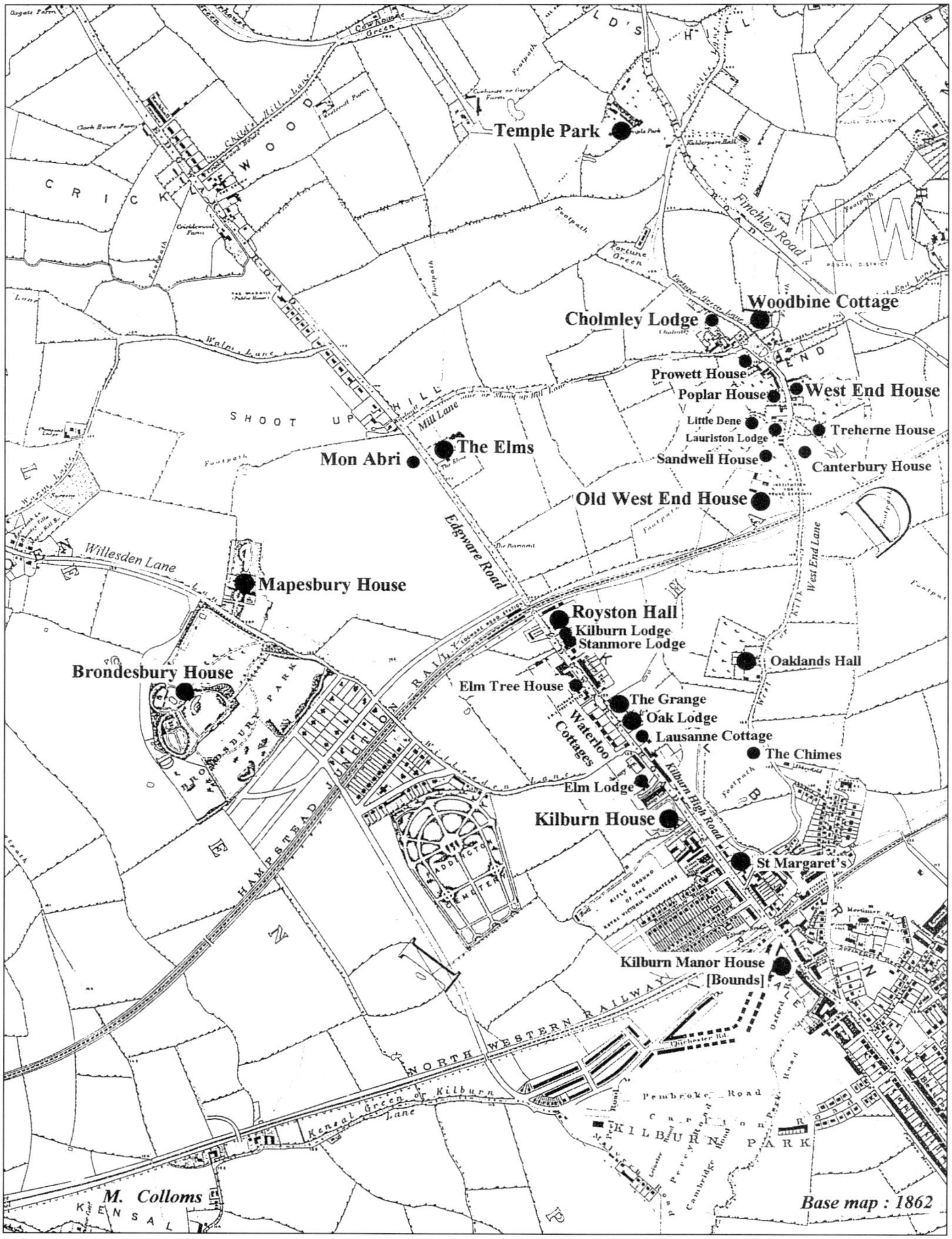

17. *A map, compiled by Marianne Colloms, showing the location of the major houses in the area.*

Kilburn Priory and extended to the parish border with neighbouring St Marylebone. Another large landholding belonged to the Powell Cotton family: this consisted of Kilburn Woods and the Liddell Farm, which lay north and west of West End Lane. On the Willesden side the main estates were those of The Manor House, the Roberts family, Brondesbury and Mapesbury.

In the following sections we will look at each of the large houses and the gentry who owned or occupied them. We will first travel north up the Willesden side of the High Road and then turn back down the Hampstead side from Shoot Up Hill, before going to West End.

BOUNDS AND THE MANOR HOUSE

The first large house to be seen on entering Kilburn from the south was the Manor House of Willesden, which occupied a site between today's Oxford and Cambridge Roads (*ill. 15*). A farmhouse was built on the Edgware Road in the late 16th century, and the estate had 160 acres of land. In 1567 the lessee and occupier, William Bovington of Kilburn, was given permission to build a house, which by 1649 had been enlarged to six rooms. In 1788 this was owned by Dame Sarah Salusbury (née Burroughs), the widow of Sir Thomas Salusbury, Judge of the High Court of the Admiralty. She settled the estate in trust for her husband's nephew, the Rev. Lynch Salusbury (later Burroughs), and when he died in 1837 it passed to his daughter Dame Elizabeth Mary Salusbury, who had married her cousin Sir Thomas Robert Salusbury.

A Major Close was rated in 1821 and William Wilberforce from 1826 to 1830. In the 1841 census it is called the 'Manor House, Kilburn' and ten years later it is shown as 'Manor Farm'. The occupants were members of the Baker family who were there from 1830 and farmed the 211 acres.

KILBURN HOUSE

This land, near today's Priory Park Road, belonged to the Roberts family who were also large land owners in Neasden and Harlesden from the 15th century. During the 17th century, Sir William Roberts was MP for Middlesex, and lived at Neasden House. He took the Parliamentary side in the Civil War, and was a member of the committee which tried King Charles I, although he did not sign the death warrant. The estate passed through successive generations of the family until Sir William Roberts sold it in 1664 to William Morgan. In 1807 Walwyn Graves, a descendant of William's, sold the Kilburn estate, consisting of a large house and six fields totalling 106 acres, to Daniel Stuart of 348 the Strand.

For most of its history Kilburn House was leased to a series of wealthy tenants, who usually stayed only a few years. In 1729 it was called 'The Great House', and was leased to the Hon. Thomas Cornwallis (it is not clear, what, if any, connection there is between this person and Lord Cornwallis, see below). From 1802 to 1810 a Paul Giblett was rated for the house and large amounts of land. Daniel Stuart himself lived at the house for about four years before selling it to the next owner-occupier, Sir Samuel Auchmuty, who was there from 1815 until his death in 1822.

Sir Samuel, a distinguished soldier, was born in New York in 1756 where his father was rector of the main Anglican church. When the American colonies declared war against England, the Auchmuty family declared their allegiance to the King, and young Samuel fought at the battles of Brooklyn and Whiteplains. After the war he came to England with his regiment, but found it impossible to live on his lieutenant's pay. From 1783 to 1797 he saw war service in India where he was promoted to lieutenant-colonel and returned with two powerful patrons in Cornwallis and Sir Robert Abercromby.

In 1800, Auchmuty took the 10th regiment to assist in subduing the French in Egypt under General Baird. Their march across the desert and passage down the Nile was a romantic story enjoyed by the public, and Auchmuty became a popular hero.

In 1806 he was put in command of the reinforcements for South America and later saw successful action against the Dutch in Java, and for these services he was made a Knight of the Bath. The peace of 1815 ended his active service and it was at this point that he moved to Kilburn House. In 1821, after being unemployed some years, Auchmuty was appointed as commander-in-chief in Ireland. However, he did not enjoy this for long as he fell dead off his horse on 11 August 1822, in Phoenix Park. He was buried in Christchurch Cathedral.

In 1839 the newspaper shop proprietor W.H. Smith, senior, bought Kilburn House, then a pleasant suburban villa in its own grounds, and this became the family home instead of the office at 192 Strand. The firm's slogan was 'First on

18. W.H. Smith MP (1825-91) who, with his father, founded the newspaper shop empire.

the Road' and Smith made his fortune by distributing newspapers all over the country faster than his rivals. When Queen Victoria came to the throne in 1839, Smith's coaches got the news across the country faster than the Royal Mail. But he became ill through overwork and the family hoped that the move to Kilburn would help him to relax. Every weekday morning at four the carriage came to take father and son to the Strand office to oversee the dispatch of papers by the early mails. The five mile journey took nearly an hour.

But the peace and tranquillity the family wanted for their father was eroded by building development which ended the seclusion of Kilburn House. As W.H. Smith junior said, 'I can't even kiss my sister without being seen from a dozen windows'. So, in 1856 the family left Kilburn and moved to Hertfordshire.

William Henry Smith was born in Duke Street, Grosvenor Square, London, on 24 June 1825. His parents were strict Methodists and the boy was educated entirely at home, except for some months in 1839 spent as a boarder at Tavistock Grammar School, where his brother-in-law was the headmaster. At sixteen he wanted to go to Oxford and prepare for holy orders, but, in deference to his father's wishes, instead he entered the news-agency house in the Strand in 1846. He opened negotiations with various railway companies for the right to open bookstalls at their stations, and in 1851 secured a monopoly of those on the London & North Western system. Because of the scrupulous care taken to exclude all salacious literature, which had made railway bookstalls notorious, young Smith got the name of 'the North-Western Missionary'.

Smith entered Parliament in 1868 and devoted himself to social questions, making his maiden speech on a motion relating to pauperism and vagrancy. He held various senior posts until 1877 when he joined the cabinet as first Lord of the Admiralty. Disraeli incurred some sharp criticism for this appointment of a London tradesman. The incongruity of the choice found popular expression in the comic opera *HMS Pinafore*, by Gilbert and Sullivan: 'Stick close to your desks and never go to sea, And you all may be ruler of the Queen's Navee!' But Smith's appointment belied all misgivings and proved a complete success.

Smith was incessantly at his post and his health was giving way under the strain. In August 1891, he moved to Walmer Castle, his official residence as warden of the Cinque Ports, and died there on 6 October 1891.

The last occupier of Kilburn House was John Farmer, of Saxby and Farmer Signal Works (*see p69*), who lived there from 1866 until 1882.

THE ELMS, AINSWORTH'S HOUSE

The Elms stood on the site of the State Cinema. At different times it was called, The Elms, Elm House, Elm Cottage or Elm Lodge (it should not be confused with 'The Elms' on the Hampstead side of Shoot Up Hill). The earliest reference we have is 1760 when a John Braint lived there. Other owners or occupants were, Lady Salusbury (1799) and from 1812 to 1823 Rev. Woodman, curate at Willesden. It was described in 1816 as, 'a house having a lawn before it surrounded by lofty elms, a garden and a fishpond'.

Mrs Pickersgill was rated for the house from 1829 until 1832. She was probably the wife of Henry William Pickersgill R.A. an eminent portrait painter, who among his many works painted the writer W.H. Ainsworth who later lived in the house. In 1830 Mrs Pickersgill was advertising 'Female Education' at Elm Lodge, Kilburn. She wished to receive:

> 'A select number of Young Ladies, whom it will be her anxious endeavour to treat with all the kindness and attention that maternal solicitude can bestow or require. Her object is

19. The Elms, Ainsworth's home, was surrounded by lofty elm trees, with a lawn between the house and the High Road. To the rear were extensive gardens and a large pond where rumour had it someone had committed suicide.

> to combine essential with elegant accomplishments, and to effect all that can be desired towards refined female education. The well-known salubrity of the spot, and its convenient distance from the metropolis, are in themselves powerful recommendations, which are greatly heightened by extensive pleasure-grounds, and a botanical garden, tastefully laid out for intellectual improvement and exercise.'

In 1832, following Mrs Pickersgill, John Ebers, a widower with two daughters moved into the house. At the time, he combined the duties of manager of the Opera House with his publishing business in Old Bond Street. In 1826 he had met a young man called William Harrison Ainsworth, who was to become his son-in-law. Ainsworth was born in Manchester in 1805, the son of a solicitor, and he followed his father's profession. But he was more interested in writing and his work began to be published in literary journals. On the death of his father in 1824, Ainsworth came to London to finish his legal education, but after meeting John Ebers he gave up the law for literature. It was Ebers who published an early work of Ainsworth's, a novel called *Sir John Chiverton*, in 1826. The same year Ainsworth married Anne Frances or 'Fanny', the youngest daughter of Ebers. They were both aged 21 and they lived at Sussex Place, Regent's Park, where John Ebers also lived. Six years later the whole family moved to Kilburn.

In 1831 Ainsworth began to write a novel called *Rookwood*. Its finest passage tells of Dick Turpin's ride to York, which is a marvel of descriptive writing. 'This feat,' he says, 'for feat it was, being the composition of a hundred novel pages in less than twenty-four hours, was achieved at The Elms, a house I then occupied at Kilburn.' The success of *Rookwood* was immediate and astonishing. The 'Jack Falstaff' inn at Kilburn where Dick Turpin met with his gang was based on The Cock, just a short walk from The Elms. While writing the book Ainsworth, a good horseman, said that he had performed the ride to York to show that it was possible. Although many of us today know the story of Dick Turpin's ride on Black Bess, we must remember that it is fictitious. Our research has found no historical evidence to link the real Dick Turpin to Kilburn at all.

Though Ainsworth's fame grew, his marriage was not successful. He separated from his wife in 1835 and moved with his three young daughters to Kensal Lodge. Ainsworth followed his *Rookwood* success by writing about another highwayman, Jack Sheppard, in two novels, entitled *Crichton* (1837) and *Jack Sheppard* (1839). In 1841 he moved next door to Kensal Manor House which became famous for its hospitality, and where Dickens, Thackeray, Landseer, Jerrold, and Cruikshank, were among his guests. He continued his successful writing career and between 1834 and 1881 published 39 novels. He died at Reigate on 3 January 1882 and was buried at Kensal Green cemetery.

In the 1851 census The Elms was occupied by the family of Mr E. Williams, who gave his occupation as, 'writer at India House'. Staying with the family was his seven-year-old nephew, Shelley Leigh Hunt, whose name suggests a link to two poets. The boy's grandfather was Edward Ellerker Williams, a captain in the East India Company, a talented artist who spent his spare time drawing the Indian scenery. He settled in Geneva where the stories about Shelley led him to seek the poet out in Pisa. From 1821 he worked closely with Shelley copying out poems for publication. His previous naval experience, combined with Shelley's passion for the sea, resulted in the construction of the ill-fated yacht, *Don Juan*, in which they both lost their lives in July 1822. Williams left a son; Edward Medwin Williams, who was the person living in Kilburn in 1851, and a daughter Rosalind who married a son of the poet Leigh Hunt and they named their son Shelley Leigh Hunt.

By 1861 the rate books show that Joshua Baker, a major landowner, farmer and hay salesman in Kilburn, had moved from Kilburn Manor House into Elm Lodge where he stayed until about 1891.

BRONDESBURY MANOR HOUSE

Travelling up the main road and turning left, on either side of Mapes or Willesden Lane as it was later called, were two very old houses. These were Brands or Brondesbury, which lay on the southern side, and Mapes or Mapesbury on the northern side.

21. A view of Kilburn High Road looking north to the corner of Willesden Lane. These buildings were on the site of today's State Cinema.

20. This shows the entrance to 'The Terrace', a small road which still exists, leading off Kilburn High Road, near today's State Cinema.

The Brondesbury Manor House estate is first mentioned in 1246, and by 1649 it consisted of over 200 acres. A moated house existed here in 1538 when it was leased to Thomas Young, a yeoman of Willesden. Generations of the Marsh family owned the property from about 1615 right through till 1749, when on the Messeder road map it is shown as an L-shaped building with a central cupola.

Towards the end of the 18th century the house was rebuilt, and by 1788, when Lady Sarah Salusbury purchased the freehold (along with Kilburn Manor House), it was a three-storied villa with a central entrance bay rising the full height of the north front, and a lower wing. In 1789, Humphry Repton, the great landscape gardener, laid out the grounds, commenting favourably on the hill-top situation and the view towards London. By 1821 it was occupied by Sir Coutts Trotter, part of the great Scottish banking family. In 1834 four acres of the estate were sold to the London & Birmingham Railway Company. The Trotter family were there until 1840, when the mansion was occupied by Lady Elizabeth Salusbury, and then Charles Hambro from 1843 to 1849. An elegant house, it had numerous occupiers, including the solicitor John Coverdale, from 1862 to 1867 when he moved across the road to Oak Lodge.

MAPESBURY

The name of this house and estate derives from Walter Map or Mapes, 'an author and wit' from Hereford who was born about 1140. In 1162 he was a clerk in the court of Henry II and travelled and worked for the King in Limoges, Anjou and Rome. He became a canon of Lincoln and in 1176 was awarded the income from the Mapesbury estate which belonged to St Paul's. His connection with the court seems to have ended with the young King's death in 1183. In 1197 Map was made archdeacon of Oxford and he died about 1210. He was a scholar, well versed in law and theology, and a writer and poet. Many authorities suggest Map as the author of Lancelot and other Arthurian romances, but his lasting reputation was as a satirist of the Church of Rome through a series of Latin poems. As a link with our present work, it is interesting to note that Leigh Hunt translated one of Map's 'Latin Drinking Songs'.

A house stood on the Mapesbury estate for a considerable time and appears in a deed of 1519. The house was neglected and in 1603 the lessee was instructed to rebuild at the landlord's expense as much of it as he thought necessary, and fill up the moat on three sides and make a new moat more distant from the house. In 1649 the 300-acre estate was itemised. It included the mansion house, stables, gatehouses, bridge-

22. Brondesbury Manor House. The gardens were laid out by Repton and the house was later the home of Lady Elizabeth Salusbury, a major landowner in the neighbourhood.

23. Mapesbury Manor House. Used in the 19th century as a horse training centre by the Anderson family.

houses, farm land and copses. The house was rebuilt late in the 17th century and had a two-storied main front of five bays.

By 1828 the house had again become dilapidated when William Anderson, a Piccadilly jobmaster, subleased the estate and made improvements to the house. William and John Anderson, father and son, used Mapesbury as a horse-training centre. In 1863 the writer Edmund Yates moved from Abbey Road and rented Mapesbury House, which was then owned by John Anderson whom he called, 'the well known horse-dealer of Green Street'. In his autobiography Yates described Mapesbury as:

> 'A capital old-fashioned house, standing in a large garden, and surrounded by a congeries of stabling and loose boxes dedicated to the comfort and well-being of Mr Anderson's highly valuable stock-in-trade. There were also a miniature farm, a tan-ride furnished with various obstacles for leaping experiments, a large staff of rough-riders, helpers etc. all within half and hour of Hyde Park Corner. It was a delightful place, but in somewhat difficult of access and not easy to find.'

To illustrate the problem he tells how John Parry, one of his friends who had taken a cab from London, knocked on the doors of three houses in Willesden Lane but nobody knew where Yates was. Parry kept calling out to the cab driver: 'Take me beyond the cemetery!' which he later thought was very amusing.

While living at Mapesbury, Yates wrote his best selling novel called *Broken to Harness*. He had seen a painting by Landseer called *The Pretty Horsebreaker*, and this together with his surroundings at Mapesbury, inspired him. The story was the life and death of Kate Mellon, the 'pretty horsebreaker', a young woman who rode to hounds. This was 'new and hitherto untrodden ground', which proved very popular with the press and public, and was praised by Dickens. Yates later said, 'If I had never lived at Mapesbury I do not believe that I would have written a novel.' Towards the end of his life he moved to a house in Kilburn Vale.

WATERLOO COTTAGES

The section of land from Willesden Lane to Dyne Road was once a farm dating back to at least 1681 when the Marsh family occupied it. In 1815 Thomas Buckley (after whom Buckley Road is named), obtained the freehold on 20 acres. Here he built seven large houses which he called Waterloo Cottages, following Wellington's victory over Napoleon. The houses were set back from the Edgware Road and each had a long garden in front. They were occupied by a number of wealthy and professional people and lasted until 1885. Joseph Peters, one of the coach building family who lived at the Grange, was there from 1851 to 1864. Sadly, no trace of these once beautiful houses exists today. Just the name is remembered by a narrow alley calledWaterloo Passage running behind the shops from Willesden Lane to Buckley and Burton Roads.

24. In addition to the seven large houses called Waterloo Cottages, Waterloo farm occupied the land to the north. The farm house was demolished to make way for Willesden Town Hall near the corner of Dyne Road and Kilburn High Road.

25. George Sala, by 'Ape', in Vanity Fair. Sala, a journalist, lived at Elm Tree House when young.

THE SALA HOME

We have to move further up the High Road to find Elm Tree House which stood at the back of the timber yard near Kilburn Brewery. This was once occupied for a short period by Madame Sala, mother of the journalist, George Augustus Sala, who lived here with her when he was a boy.

George was the youngest of thirteen children, only five of whom survived. A few weeks after George's birth his father died also, leaving Madame Sala to cope with bringing up the children. She did so by giving singing lessons from 11 to 4 each day. Aged about four George was blinded from an attack of measles, but later regained his sight.

Madame Sala lived in Brighton for six months of the year, spent three months in London and the other three months in great country houses as a guest and a singing teacher. In his autobiography George says that as a young child they, 'lived in Brighton, but spent "temporary villeggiature" at Clapham, at Richmond and at Kilburn' in the mid 1830s. They moved to nearby Cricklewood where they rented 'a delightful country cottage but which I suppose, by this time has altogether passed into the semi-detached villa stage of existence'. There were frequent performances of private theatricals, 'the stage being in the back drawing room and the auditorium in the front'. George remembers that between the acts of one of the dramas, the wonderfully named Mr Rippamonti played the overture to *Der Freischutz* on his chin. The only other memory Sala has of Cricklewood is that the potman at The Crown was a Negro with a wooden leg. The young Sala was very impressed that the man had been a cymbal player in one of the regiments of Foot Guards at the battle of Waterloo. By 1837 the family was staying at a house in Pine-apple Villas in Maida Vale, not far from Kilburn. George recalls that in an empty house, next door, a notorious murder took place. James Greenacre, who was caught three months later, killed a woman and then took her dismembered body to different parts of London. While travelling on an omnibus with the head in a canvas bag on his knees, Greenacre said to the conductor that 'by right he ought to pay for two passengers'.

Elm Tree House appears in local directories up to 1881. Today a short passage called Drakes Yard leads from the High Road into the site of the Timber Yard, but there are no remains of the house.

MON ABRI, SHOOT UP HILL

Mon Abri, or 27 Shoot Up Hill, was a house on the Willesden side, now demolished. This was for a many years the residence of a well-known centenarian Senor Manuel Garcia, who was born in Madrid in 1805. His father trained him for the opera using the rather unusual method of suddenly pinching him to produce the high notes. Garcia became a great teacher of singing, and the world famous Jenny Lind was one of his pupils. Garcia also invented the laryngoscope (a mirror arrangement to examine the throat). On his 100th birthday he was received by Edward VII at Buckingham Palace and decorated as Hon. Commander of the Victorian Order. He was still regularly giving lessons at the house when he

26. Mon Abri, Shoot Up Hill, the home for many years of Senor Manuel Garcia, a renowned singing teacher.

was called the 'oldest singing teacher in the world'. He died at Mon Abri on 1 July 1906 and was buried in a Roman Catholic cemetery near Woking.

At this point in our journey we cross the road to the Hampstead side, and starting at Shoot Up Hill, work our way back down through Kilburn before moving along West End Lane to look at the houses there.

THE ELMS

The Powell Cotton family owned a substantial amount of land in Kilburn and West Hampstead, on both sides of West End Lane. Their largest property was a farm bordering Shoot Up Hill which they bought from the Liddell family in 1773, its fields reaching north to the parish boundary with Hendon and across to Hampstead Cemetery. The remote farm buildings stood roughly where St Cuthbert's Road is today. The Froggatt family leased the farm in 1786, and enjoyed an unusually long tenancy of over sixty years, up to John Froggatt who died in 1850. No farmer in the true sense of the word would ever occupy the farmhouse again.

The new tenants were two brothers, William and George Verey, who were local brewers. As they were also leasing the adjoining Ripley fields, it meant that for a while they were running some 160 acres of meadow on the Hampstead side of the road in addition to Kilburn Brewery and other property on the Willesden side. George's 21-year lease of the house was up in 1872 and the new occupant was also the owner of the estate, which he had inherited from his uncle in 1849. Captain Henry Perry Cotton was the black sheep of the family. He had served in the 7th Bengal Cavalry and married the daughter of his regimental commander. But the couple were unhappy and Henry set up home with his mistress, Charlotte, instead. They were finally able to marry when Henry's wife died in 1868. The couple did not, or more likely could not, live at Quex Park, the family home in Kent, and The Elms seemed a good compromise. Henry promptly renamed the house 'Kingsgate Lodge' after the village in Kent where he spent his childhood.

ROYSTON HALL

The next house about ten minutes walk down the Edgware Road, was owned by the Ripley family. Another converted farmhouse, its fields stretched right across to the village of West End. In 1784 a 21-year lease was taken out by Samuel Brawne, a coachmaster who owned the Coach and Horses Inn, off the Strand. He was the grandfather of Fanny Brawne, with whom John Keats fell in love. She was born in 1800 in nearby West End. As a boy, George 'Beau' Brummell visited his aunt, Jane Brawne, at the farm house where 'he ate so much of her delicious damson tart that he could eat no more – yet he enjoyed it so much that he could not bear to leave off, and consequently broke into howls of tearful frustration'.

In 1813 the new tenant was Major Close (*see p.23*). Subsequent events indicate that Close was either the owner or chief stockholder in the (Great) Westminster Dairy Company. In 1826 he went into business with William Wilberforce, the eldest son of the great statesman of the same name. William junior took over the remainder of the lease from Close.

The letters of Wilberforce senior, reveal that William had been a problematical son, leaving Cambridge under a cloud in 1819 and next abandoning a promising career at the bar due to ill health. Together with his wife and son,

William junior moved into Highwood Hill, his father's new home at Mill Hill. But then he met Major Close. Wilberforce loaned his son the money he needed to invest in Close's dairy company. But not only did the company fail to make a profit, it soon went heavily into debt and by December 1828 William was in deep financial difficulties, and asked his father for a further £6,000. William senior was forced to borrow the money.

But it was already too late, for the dairy company was well and truly on the rocks. In March 1830 Wilberforce was warned that far from being an honourable man, Close was a rogue. Close left the business soon after – 'circumstances of a very suspicious nature have since come to view' – and in November 1830 William junior and his family sailed for Italy to avoid his creditors. He owed upwards of fifty thousand pounds, equivalent to several million pounds in today's money! Presumably Major Close had made certain that all transactions were in his partner's name. Rather than let William remain a penniless exile, Wilberforce took over his son's debts. He even managed to joke about the situation: 'I wish William would keep company with his father instead of his cows. It would be quite as profitable and much more agreeable'. Declining all offers of help, Wilberforce senior set about raising the money. He sold Highwood Hill as well as land he owned in Yorkshire and ate deep into his capital. Following his death three years later, his widow was left with a meagre annuity and no home. Seemingly William never took responsibility for his parents' plight and always denied he had 'engaged in a speculation unfitting to my station which proved so ruinous to my father's fortune as to compel him to break up his establishment'.

The farmhouse was christened 'Royston Hall' after an unmarried lady of that name, who stayed there just a year or two. In 1836 the land was leased by William and George Verey, the brothers who later took over the adjoining Powell Cotton fields. They had established the Kilburn Brewery on a site almost opposite the entrance to Royston Hall. They were not very interested in the house, which they never occupied, but used the land, which they leased for the next thirty years, and the farm yard, where they built a malt house. Royston Hall became a girls' school under Harriet Scarborough and when she left in 1842 the building was subdivided to provide two homes, the larger part retaining the name Royston Hall with the southern and much smaller wing called Royston Lodge. A series of

27. Kilburn Lodge and Stanmore Cottage, showing the buildings marked up for sale and eventual demolition. They stood on Kilburn High Road, opposite Kilburn Brewery.

28. The Grange, Kilburn High Road, from the garden. The building was demolished in c.1910.

short-term lets came to an end when both stood empty in the spring of 1859. This was hardly surprising, as the Hampstead Junction Railway was building on an embankment just a few yards away and was due to open in the following year. But there were tenants who were willing to put up with a railway in the back garden until the estate was sold for building to the British Land Company in 1868.

THE GRANGE

Samuel Ware, who was also architect to the Duke of Devonshire and designed the Burlington Arcade, Piccadilly, also built The Grange and neighbouring Oak Lodge as a speculative venture.

Completed by January 1831, the early title of 'Gothic House' was soon superseded by 'The Grange', the name given by its long-term owners, the Peters family who occupied it from 1843. Thomas Peters was a well-known coachbuilder whose workshops were off the Edgware Road near Marble Arch, while his showrooms were at 95-96 Park Street, Grosvenor Square. His workmanship was of the highest quality, and he displayed work at the 1851 Great Exhibition at the Crystal Palace and made coaches for Queen Victoria. Peters was born in Reigate about 1786 and he died in 1863 leaving the business to his eldest son, John Winpenny Peters. His son took over the house in 1863, purchasing first the freehold and then adding a neighbouring market garden a few years later. Following Ware's death, Peters bought The Grange in 1867. In 1882 the *Kilburn Times* reported his death at The Grange where the coffin lay for people to pay their respects and 200 of the Peters employees, past and present, filed through the room. At the funeral, the large cortège, including the state coach of the Lord Mayor, attracted much attention in Kilburn.

Until the house was sold in 1910, his widow Mrs Ada Britannia Peters was the owner and occupier. She was called 'Lady' Peters by the locals, but this was only a courtesy title. It was rumoured that she had been an actress or professional vocalist before her marriage. She held lavish garden parties at the house, one of her guests being Oliver de Lorncourt, the Marquis de Leuville, a composer of songs and poems. The British Library lists five books of his poems composed between 1867 and 1889, which were well received by the public. However, Henry Labouchère, who carried out a crusade against impostors in his journal *Truth* laid bare the mock Marquis. He was probably born plain Tom Oliver, and he may have worked as a hairdresser's assistant before marrying a French woman called

29. Items from the Sale Catalogue for The Grange in 1910.

de Leuville. He then appeared as a Marquis in London society. After his exposure by *Truth* he lay low for some time, but he managed to return with financial support from Mrs Peters. He was the centre of attraction at The Grange where Mrs Peters established a literary salon. Journalists were sent invitations that arrived in Fleet Street like 'a shower of snow'. To some she was a merry widow, while others more harshly called her a 'giddy relic'. With the support of Mrs Peters, The 'Marky' took a suite of rooms in Victoria Street where he gave receptions, which Willie Wilde, the brother of Oscar, would often attend. Journalists recall the Marky's visits to their offices where 'he left in his trail the scent of attar of roses which for days would overcome the sub-editors'.

It seems likely Mrs Peters' relationship with the Marky lasted until de Leuville's death in France in 1908. This might explain why Ada was so rarely mentioned in local papers and despite

30. The Grange laid out as a park. A similar postcard of the same period has the following message: 'At last I am sending a few cards. I can't get a very choice selection, as Kilburn is not a particularly pretty place, but I will get a few more next week. The Grange pictures are new to you, as that is a new place since the old place was pulled down. I could not get one of the cinema yet, but I hope you will soon come over to see for yourself. The war still seems to be going strong, but I guess old Kaiser Bill won't realise the height of his ambition, nunno. Joe has got in the Royal Fusiliers and is at Colchester now, hopes to go to the Front soon.

her long-term ownership of The Grange, the fact that her death merited only a cursory obituary, lacking any of the usual detailed biographical information. She died in 1910 and was buried in Kensal Green cemetery with the rest of the Peters family.

In May 1910 *The Times* carried a letter calling for a Kilburn Open Space fund to obtain the grounds of The Grange as a park. In 1911 Hampstead Council (with the aid of Willesden Council) bought the Grange grounds for £19,500 (only £600 had been raised by pubic subscription) and opened it as Grange Park, but efforts to preserve the house failed and it was pulled down. Earlier, Sir Oswald Stoll proposed to erect a Coliseum, on the lines of his London theatre in St Martin's Lane, on the part of the estate fronting Kilburn High Road, but his application to the LCC for a music and dancing licence was opposed by Hampstead Council. Finally, the Grange Cinema was opened on the site on 30 July 1914.

OAK LODGE

Samuel Ware built this house in 1830 and let it to Samuel Brazier who stayed only a few years. The second tenant was John Coverdale who named the house Oak Lodge when he moved from Brondesbury House in 1834; he stayed until 1862. He was a solicitor with a partnership in Gray's Inn. Between 1863 and 1875 Frederick James Clark was the owner and occupier having bought the property in 1867 after Samuel Ware's death. Clark was much involved in Hampstead affairs, as he was the land agent for the Maryon Wilson estate for 25 years, while his brother Alfred Clark was the Steward of the Manor. A sizeable increase in rateable value indicates he made substantial improvements to the Lodge. In addition to all the usual living space, Oak Lodge had a master bedroom suite plus a further thirteen bedrooms, a billiard room, library and school room. It was Clark who bought the neighbouring Lausanne Cottage, using it for his coachman. This astute move and Clark's later purchase of a field bordering his back fence and reaching across to West End Lane, transformed what had been a small estate into a sizeable twelve acre property with considerable development potential that included frontages to two main roads.

The last owner and occupier between 1877 and 1878 was Jacob Francis Hirsch who seems to have been a property developer. In 1881 the land was auctioned off, and local developers Thomas Bate and Richard Pincham bought many of the building plots. By 1883 the house was gone and the whole area was redeveloped as Messina and Gascony Ave.

LAUSANNE COTTAGE

Tradition has it that this house, opposite Willesden Lane, was a 17th-century hunting lodge for Charles II, and even that Nell Gwynne lived there for a while, but like so many stories of this nature, there is absolutely no proof. What

31. Lausanne Cottage, which stood roughly opposite Willesden Lane. It was wrongly thought to be an old hunting lodge.

is certain is that by the middle of the next century there was a farmhouse here, serving a farm whose fields reached back to West End Lane and the fringes of West End village. Lausanne Cottage was probably a new build occupying part if not all of the site of the old farmhouse. The new house was 'a quaint-looking old building, mainly of wood, with a high-pointed roof'. The appearance might explain why locals believed it had been the old hunting lodge. The first occupant from 1826 to 1831 was Samuel Rogers, the surgeon. In 1826 young John Pocock recorded in his diary that the two Miss Rogers, daughters of the family doctor, called in the evening to play whist. The following year, mad with toothache, John ran from his house to the village to Dr Rogers, but he would not extract it. Charles Watson, a stockbroker, and his son were the next occupants until the Cottage and its grounds were absorbed into the neighbouring Oak Lodge property.

THE LIDDELL ESTATE

The last farmhouse on Edgware Road stood just north of West End Lane, on the southern edge of its fields that bordered the Lane. The farm was owned by the Liddell family who sold it to the Powell Cottons. The lessee for much of the nineteenth century was William Baker, a local man, born in Wembley. He became a major farmer in the neighbourhood, renting land on both sides of Edgware Road, including Kilburn Woods, Hall Oak Farm (reaching from Frognal down to his Kilburn land), Belsize Farm and Willesden Manor farm. On the 1851 census he said he was running 290 acres of land but only employed 6 labourers, indicating the low maintenance needed to farm grassland.

A brick house was built alongside the farmyard – William's son Henry was married to a lady called Margaret, which is probably how 'St Margaret's Cottage' got its name. The neighbouring farmhouse had become very dilapidated, probably because Baker preferred to run his Hampstead land from the Hall Oak farmhouse in Frognal. But now he took the decision to redevelop the site and transfer his offices to Kilburn. By 1849 a new farmhouse complete with stables and outbuildings stood on the north corner of what would later become Birchington Road. William Baker retired or died soon after and the properties were taken over by his son Henry and his grandson Joshua. In 1865 the Powell Cottons began building on their Kilburn land, which meant that Baker's income fell as the farmland progressively declined in area. As Henry and Joshua were already established estate agents and surveyors, the family were well prepared for changing times and a full time move into property and house sales. They continued to live in the rebuilt but increasingly redundant farmhouse now called Brondesbury House, until the last of the land they were renting reverted to the Powell Cottons. It eventually became the offices of Joshua Baker and Wilkinson auctioneers, (originally Baker and Sons).

The history of St Margaret's is less straightforward. The last owner and occupier was builder Robert Allen Yerbury who rented the house about 1877. He soon bought the freehold as well as a large chunk of land adjoining his grounds and built Colas Mews (now behind Woolworth's). He next used the garden in front of the renamed St Margaret's Lodge as the site for a terrace of shops. Finally he established steam sawing, planing and moulding mills, plus yards and sheds for the storage and seasoning of timber on West End Lane behind the Lodge, and all without demolishing the house! St Margaret's was left hemmed in by noise, dirt and buildings, separated from a crowded mews by a low wall, with no proper garden or carriage drive. Its front windows now faced the rear of a row of shops along the High Street with only a narrow passageway to give access to the main road. Who would want to live in a house like that? Amazingly Yerbury found a series of tenants in the 1880s before moving back into St Margaret's Lodge himself. And there he stayed until he died in 1894.

ALONG WEST END LANE

West End Lane is one of the district's oldest roads. It is possible to trace most of its bends and twists from the earliest maps on the modern street plan. As late as the 1860s it was still a true country lane with high banks, 'hedged irregularly for a greater part of its length, and enshrined too by the embracing branches of the majestic oak, elm and other forest trees, through which a sunny gleam here and there broke'. However, this idyllic description disappeared whenever it rained hard, because in the absence of any drainage, the sunken earth roadway turned into a quagmire. Leading out of the Edgware Road it wound its way north to the village of West End before turning abruptly east to climb the hill to Hampstead. It was so secluded that

Queen Victoria liked to drive out and enjoy a peaceful walk among the hedgerows. Locals even called the lower end of the Lane 'The Queens Road' after their prestigious visitor who would sometimes drive as far as the outskirts of West End to visit her friend Colonel Orde. The neighbouring fields were used for grazing stock and the artist Edwin Landseer, of Trafalgar Square lions' fame, is recorded as attempting his first youthful sketches of livestock here.

While a few large houses had been built along Kilburn High Road and in the village of West End, the surrounding neighbourhood provided ample scope for a wealthy man to build his own, sometimes creating an extensive estate in the process. A new 'gentry' class predominated, men who had made their money by working rather than inheriting it from their parents. The district was firmly in the country but close enough to Town to permit commuting, although in some cases, their villas and mansions were used purely as holiday homes.

THE CHIMES

The artist John Rogers Herbert purchased his two-acre plot at the corner of the Lane and the newly formed Quex Road in 1867 (*see p.127*). He may have chosen the site because a Roman Catholic Order was buying the land next door. In December 1866 Herbert had attended the stone laying ceremony for the temporary Chapel and subsequently planned his new home so he could see the Light burning before the Blessed Sacrament when the Church was completed. Herbert called his home The Chimes after the Dickens novel of the same name, and both house and church were designed by architect Edwin Welby Pugin.

OAKLANDS

Charles Spain, a prosperous butcher, was already leasing the grazing land he bought from Ware in 1824. He completed a substantial brick house, called York Villa, set back a short distance from the Lane by January 1826, but did not live long to enjoy it. It lay in landscaped grounds on the west side of the Lane, on the site of today's Cotleigh and Dynham Roads. The house next passed to a series of tenants. Mr Francis Truefitt, 'the greatest of all barbers', took a short lease on the property in the 1830s. The Truefitt family had several shops for hairdressing and perfumery in Old Bond Street, New Bond Street and the Burlington Arcade, while Francis was wigmaker to King George IV. From 1856 to 1859 Charles Asprey resided there. In 1847 he had opened a shop at 166 New Bond Street as a Stationers and Dressing Case Manufacturers. Real fame came to Asprey in 1861 with his appointment to Victoria and Albert for dressing cases, writing cases and jewellery, and it is of course for the latter that Asprey and Company is renowned today.

32. Oaklands Hall, the home of Donald Nicoll and Sir Charles Murray. On the left is the Lodge; the house, hidden by trees, is to the rear.

Donald Nicoll was the new tenant in 1860. A man with a finger in several lucrative financial pies, over the next decade he purchased the house, added more land and transformed the villa into a palatial mansion set in extensive landscaped grounds. With his brother he was a partner in H.J. and D. Nicoll, who began trading as army outfitters. By the 1840s the firm had progressed to general men's tailoring and set up shop in fashionable Regent Street, with branches in the City, Birmingham, Manchester and Liverpool. In addition to his commercial source of income, Nicoll invested heavily in land both here and in the Vale of Health, where he built the Suburban Hotel.

Nicoll served briefly as a Liberal MP and as Sheriff of London. He was a very active campaigner against capital punishment, especially after seeing the public execution of Courvoiseur, butler to Lord William Russell, who had 'plotted his murder to get back to Switzerland with his master's plate'. Nicoll was travelling by public coach from Charing Cross to Cambridge when the coachman, encouraged by most of the passengers, wedged his way into the crowd in front of the scaffold at Newgate. The jeering and abuse of the mob and the cheering of Calcraft, the public executioner, who bowed to the crowd, greatly upset Nicoll. The scene remained vividly in his memory till 1891, when he wrote a book called *Man's Revenge,* in which he called for the abolition of the death penalty. Nicoll was not alone in this, his friend Charles Dickens also wrote strongly against hanging.

In 1872 Nicoll sold Oaklands to its last occupant Sir Charles Murray (1806-1895). As a young man Murray travelled widely in America, including an expedition up the Hudson River when his companion was the American writer Fenimore Cooper. In Virginia, Murray was most upset and angry about the slavery that he saw.

In 1835, after almost dying from cholera, he was having dinner with the officers at Fort Leavenworth, the most westerly military outpost of the US. Army, when 150 Pawnee Indians arrived suddenly. Though they had never seen white men before, they shook hands, sipped Madeira and smoked cigars.

He returned to England and in July 1837 he took up a post in Windsor as Groom in Waiting to Queen Victoria, having driven some American ponies at speed from London to Windsor as a present to the young Queen. In 1845 he took up a post in Naples as Secretary to the British Legation, moving in 1846 to Egypt as Consul General. It was here that he had the Pasha capture a hippo calf and bring it several hundred miles to Cairo. It travelled to England by steamship and arrived in London Zoo on 25 May 1850. This was the first hippo ever seen in England and attracted great crowds. It lived for 23 years during which time Murray visited it frequently shouting to him in Arabic, the hippo always recognised him and replied with loud grunts.

In 1872, looking for a house to retire to, he bought Oaklands from Donald Nicoll. Murray had it enlarged to take his large collection of books and prints and then retired there on a pension of £1,300 in 1874. He spent his time writing and visiting the health spas of Europe. After several happy years Murray decided to leave Kilburn, and Thomas Bate (*see p.130*), who acted as their agent, found a Windsor property for Sir Charles. Still travelling, Murray died suddenly while visiting Paris in 1895.

All these mansions were nineteenth century creations. Before they existed, a traveller turning off Edgware Road along West End Lane would have journeyed through open fields before passing any buildings. Near the present junction with Broadhurst Gardens, the Lane took a sharp curve to the left to run right past the front door of Old West End House.

OLD WEST END HOUSE

The house stood on the slopes of a low hill, the very name signifying its links with the nearby village. Dating from the mid-seventeenth century, it was one of the oldest 'gentry' homes of the district. The original timber building was soon replaced by a more substantial brick one and the estate enlarged to include fields on both sides of the Lane.

In 1796 the property passed into the hands of the Beckford family which had lived there since 1775. William Beckford senior (1709-1770), was twice Lord Mayor of London in the 1750s. He inherited a fortune from sugar plantations in Jamaica. Contrary to popular tradition he never lived in the house, but his widow Maria did. Beckford's son William Beckford junior, wrote a best selling book called *Vathek* in 1782 (a bit like the *Arabian Nights*). The following year he married Lady Margaret Gordon, daughter of the 4th Earl of Aboyne. But sadly she died in 1786, a few days after giving birth to Susan, their second daughter.

33. William Beckford jnr, author of the novel Vathek and builder of Fonthill Abbey.

Beckford was publicly disgraced in 1784 after the newspapers carried allegations of a homosexual affair with the young William Courtenay, the Earl of Devon. This was still a capital offence under an old statute of Henry VIII, and Beckford was lucky not to have been executed. Modern historians have been unable to substantiate whether a homosexual act occurred or not, but is more likely to have been a trumped up charge by Lord Loughborough, the guardian of Courtenay. As a result of the scandal, the family insisted that the girls, Margaret and Susan, were not brought up under the same roof as Beckford, and they lived at West End House with a Swiss Calvinist governess and their grandmother, Mrs Beckford, until her death in 1789.

West End House was occupied by the Beckford family from 1775 to 1812. In his old age William Beckford always came to London for the season, and he would often ride up the Edgware Road to gaze at the old house at West End.

In 1811, Margaret, Beckford's eldest daughter, eloped with General James Orde. Beckford was furious, as he considered Orde a poor match for his daughter – Orde came from a Northumberland family of clergymen. Beckford called her 'Mrs Ordure' and threatened to cut off Margaret's inheritance, but it appears that she received £10,000 from her grandmother, Maria Beckford, and the house at West End. General Orde lived in the house from 1838-1841.

By 1842 the mansion had expanded to three storeys, with nine rooms on the top floor, presumably used by live-in servants, with seven on the floor below. The landscaped grounds included a melon ground and vinery. The tenant on the night of the 1851 census was Admiral Sartorius, when the house provided ample accommodation for eight members of his family, plus six servants and two visitors. As a young man Sartorius had served at Trafalgar and later he was Commander of the 20-gun *Slaney* in company with the *Bellerophon* when Bonaparte surrendered on board.

Between 1856-1857 Daniel Whittle Harvey was the owner/occupier. He was Commissioner of the City of London Police from 1840 till his death. Harvey established several newspapers, including the *Sunday Times* (1822) and *Weekly True Sun* (1833). He was tried at the Guildhall in 1823 for libelling George IV in an article in the *Sunday Times*, found guilty and sentenced to a fine of £200 and imprisonment in the Marshalsea for three months. He died at 26 Old Jewry, (the administrative headquarters of the City of London Police) in 1863.

SANDWELL AND CANTERBURY HOUSES

Some land lying north of Old West End House was sold to provide the site of two new villas that faced each other across West End Lane.

Completed in 1862, Sandwell House and Canterbury House were built by two close friends, John Marrian and William Greenwood. The families were neighbours in Park Road off Haverstock Hill, then moved to adjoining homes in Mansfield Villas on Rosslyn Hill. The noise and vibration from the Hampstead Junction Railway which passed under the houses drove them to seek the quiet sanctuary of West End, but in the event it was to prove a move straight from the frying pan into the fire. Marrian and Greenwood were successful business men and seemingly named their new homes after the birthplaces of their wives. Mrs Marrian was born in Birmingham, hence 'Sandwell' and Mrs Greenwood in Kent, so 'Canterbury.' Described by a local resident 'as in the Italian style of architecture with square towers', the white stucco houses apparently looked very alike. The bombshell dropped a year or so after the families took up residence. Parliament passed the Midland Railway Bill, sanctioning a line that would pass south of but uncomfortably close to the bottom of both back gardens. Mr Marrian and Mr Greenwood decided to sell to the railway company and by 1865 both families had left West End. Sandwell House was sold to the Burgess family who owned land north of Fortune Green, while Canterbury House was bought by Mr Fletcher, the owner of neighbouring Treherne House.

Fletcher first let Canterbury House to John Smith and then Anthony Lister. They were in business as 'wholesale straw hat and bonnet manufacturers, artificial flowers, ostrich and fancy feather merchants'. One of the largest firms in the country, Lister made a fortune by cornering a market specific to the period, when wearing hats was essential to fashion and respectability.

A local resident, with a countryman's eye for livestock, recalled Lister's horses rather than the man himself.

> 'I remember Mr Lister best for his imposing carriages and horses. Every day while he was in residence he drove in state to his offices in Cannon Street, and I often used to wait on purpose to see the iron gates flung open and the carriage and pair come swiftly through, with the old red-apple-faced, grey whiskered coachman and the upright young footman, in their light-fawn uniforms and cockaded hats sitting high up on the box.'

Lister died in 1896, leaving over £134,000. He is buried in Hampstead Cemetery.

TREHERNE HOUSE

North of Lister's property stood Treherne House, another of the old buildings of West End. It took its name from a field behind the house, Trehern Croft. It was an awkward, funnel shaped property, with a narrow entrance off West End Lane leading to the house and its triangular shaped grounds. In 1813 the new owner Thomas Bean

34. Treherne House, the home of the Shout family.

demolished the existing buildings and set his new mansion further back from the main road.

In 1821 the owner was Robert Shout. He was a sculptor immortalised in lines by Shelley, a personal friend, when describing Leigh Hunt's studio as: 'No doubt, Is still adorned by many a cast from Shout'. A Master of the Masons' Company and a modeller for Wedgwood, Shout was based in Holborn. His work can be found in many churches, including Temple Church, London. Robert left West End for a few years. When he returned his son Charles Lutwyche came too, but elected not to share the family home, preferring instead a more modest house overlooking the village green. When Robert died in 1843, Charles moved into Treherne House; his son Robert Howard was an architect who exhibited at the Royal Academy on several occasions. Charles' widow sold the property to its last owner, John Samuel Fletcher, who moved to West End in 1865.

Born in Manchester, the son of a merchant, Fletcher improved and named the house. As a young man in his late twenties, Fletcher was called to the bar in 1868, but only three years later, he described himself in the census as a 'barrister, not practising'. He may have suffered from general ill health but enjoyed a good private income to support his lifestyle. Locally his list of appointments seems never ending – he was a trustee of Hampstead Church and of the Wells and Campden Charity, a JP, Chairman of the Board of Guardians, to name but a few. He contributed generously to many local causes, in particular to save The Grange in Kilburn and West End Green as open spaces. A vestryman, he served as a member of the LCC and was elected Hampstead's Unionist MP, 1905-1918. He was strongly criticised for supporting women's suffrage. He was described as:

> 'A spare scholarly little man, (he walked) with a slight stoop. He had a well-trimmed iron-grey beard, a rather weather-beaten complexion, and I never remember seeing him wear anything but a well-cut grey frock coat and the shiniest of top hats. He wore the two ends of his tie, not knotted in any way, but threaded through a plain gold ring, and this left the gold collar stud exposed. The ties were sometimes a little vivid in hue.'

Fletcher married late in life 'surprising everyone' as a local put it. His bride was Sara Clark, and in 1895 they were married in Beaconsfield, near her home. He was knighted in 1919, but by then the couple had moved away and were living in Virginia Water. Fletcher died in 1924 aged 83 and appropriately enough, considering his long association with the neighbourhood, he was buried in Hampstead Churchyard. He left an estate worth over £46,000 (about £900,000 in today's money). At the time there were many and not always apocryphal stories, about people in comas being buried alive. Fletcher took detailed precautions to prevent this happening to him. He refused burial and instead stipulated his cremation should take place four days after his death but no earlier, and that a doctor examine his body to make absolutely sure he was dead before the service went ahead.

LAURISTON LODGE

Across the road from Treherne House stood Lauriston Lodge, a hotch potch of cottages joined and extended to make a single house facing, but set back from, the Lane behind a curved carriageway. In 1797, the northernmost cottage was rented to Germain Lavie who occupied and purchased all but one over the next fifteen years, adding a coach house and stables. Lauriston Lodge was separated from the next villa, Gothic Lodge, by a footpath known locally as Sweetbriar Walk. This provided the residents with a short cut across the fields to Edgware Road. Little Dene, a more secluded mansion, stood a little way down this path.

Lauriston Lodge and Little Dene have been the source of much confusion, seemingly the result of an incorrect identification made on the 1860s' Ordnance Survey. This labelled Little Dene as Lauristone (an alternative spelling) Lodge, and once in print, the error persisted down the years.

Lavie was a man of means, a property speculator and JP for Hampstead. He was a member of the consortium that purchased the lease of Belsize Manor in 1807, later selling his share. He was actively involved in the local dispute over West End Fair. A good friend and neighbour was the engraver Josiah Boydell: both men were members of the local, but nonetheless exclusive, Hampstead Dinner and Hampstead Union Clubs.

Lavie stayed at Lauriston Lodge until his death in 1825 when the property was inherited by his family and rented out. It seems Germain Lavie did not name the house; this honour is down to the first tenant, Peter Lawrie, who called it 'Lawrieston' Lodge', although the name was later altered to 'Lauriston'. Mr Lawrie made some

35. Lauriston Lodge, showing the rear of the building. It illustrates the group of cottages which were combined to form a single dwelling house.

improvements to the property, creating a twenty-room residence, not including kitchen, brew house, dairy and other domestic offices. The tallest of the buildings was probably the one described by a local resident as built of red brick, with some fine stained glass windows. Once his lease was up in 1840, the Lavie family sold the house to Sir William Woods.

Woods was only destined to enjoy his new home for a couple of years but during that time he was probably West End's best known resident. His official role was that of 'Knight Garter, Principal King of Arms and Knight of the Royal Hanoverian Guelphic Order' and he would have been well known to the villagers as the man who crowned Queen Victoria. It was reported that his funeral procession in 1842 stretched from the Lodge as far as Frognal Lane. Sir William was buried in St John's, Hampstead at his own request. An old friend of the Reverend White, the vicar of St John's, Sir William was interred in the reverend's own vault. There is a plaque to his memory inside the church.

An auction of the house's contents following the death of an elderly tenant in 1876 gives an insight into what the well furnished house of the time would contain:

'Laurieston Lodge West-end Hampstead Capital Modern Furniture comprising carved drawing-room suite covered in crimsoned figured satin, ebonised cabinets massively mounted in ormolu, walnut, rosewood, mahogany tables, a handsome eight light cut glass chandelier, plaster figures and busts, bronzes, clocks, and other decorative ornaments, mahogany dining-room and library appointments, including extending dining-table and noble pedestal sideboard with plate glass back, sarcophagus, cottage pianoforte, musical box, console, pier and chimney-glasses, valuable paintings and engravings, Brussels, Kidderminster and felt carpets, the usual bedchamber appendages including mahogany winged and other wardrobes, carved Arabian and iron bedsteads, feather and other beds, the numerous kitchen requisites, a Kent's patent knife-cleaning machine, patent mangle and refrigerator, garden roller, mowing machine and other implements, town-built Victoria (nearly new) and table appurtenances.'

The next tenant moved in almost immediately. The son of an architect and surveyor, Eugenius Birch chose civil engineering as a career and went on to specialise in that very Victorian phenomenon – the seaside pier. He created at least twelve, including the famous West Pier at Brighton, where he also constructed a sea-water aquarium. Building its large tanks and solving the resulting problems of high water pressure was something that had never been successfully tackled before. He died at Lauriston Lodge in 1884.

LITTLE DENE

Before entering the village proper, a short distance down Sweetbriar Walk stood Little Dene, built and lived in by its owner for upwards of thirty years. The Ripley brothers inherited their property in 1814, and like the Ware estate which ran along its southern border, their fields reached across to the Edgware Road. The farmland was split in two, the Kilburn end passing to Thomas Hyde Ripley, while his younger brother Jeremy Jephson had the West End land. Content to rent out most of his fields, by 1831 Jeremy, who worked as a clerk in the Customs Service, had decided to make the village his home.

Jeremy never married and on his death in 1864 the property passed to his nephew, Thomas Tyndale Ripley who also inherited the Kilburn lands a year later under his father's will. Thomas had been living in the West End house for some years. He probably used his inheritance to retire from his post in the War Department and make improvements to the villa which he rechristened Little Dene.

POPLAR HOUSE

Poplar House was one of the older properties in the village. It stood back from the Lane a little way down the present Inglewood Road, in extensive but awkwardly shaped grounds. Josiah Boydell moved here from Highgate in 1783. A well known publisher and engraver, he had been in business with his uncle John since the 1760s. But he was also a talented portrait and historical painter on his own account, with several of his works exhibited at the Royal Academy. Boydell was an active member of both local and London Society: he held dinner parties at West End attended by the likes of Lady Hamilton and was the chosen confidant of wealthy Maria Beckford when her son was in trouble. But he also worked to help the poor by establishing a new parish workhouse and was largely responsible for

36. Little Dene. A painting by the owner, J.J. Ripley, showing a wisteria covered, two-storey red-brick building on a slight rise and set back a short distance from Sweetbriar Walk.

37. Alderman John Boydell, Josiah's uncle, the engraver, who embarked on the ambitious project to produce an illustrated Shakespeare.

enlisting a local defence force, the Loyal Hampstead Association (later known as the Loyal Volunteers). Created in 1798 with a possible French invasion in mind the volunteers were also meant to help the authorities in the case of any civil disturbance. 'After a strenuous day on Hampstead Heath, the members adjourned to the captain's house at West End to feast and drink healths and sing loyal songs'.

But by this time Boydell was in financial trouble. His uncle had decided to produce an edition of Shakespeare illustrated by commissioned paintings. The plans were laid at a dinner party at Poplar House in 1796.

> 'Boydell told us to-day that the first idea of publishing their edition of Shakespeare was started at his house at West-end Hampstead, when Alderman Boydell, [Josiah's uncle] - West, – Romney, [both artists] Hayley, [the poet)] –Braithwaite [of the Post Office], Hoole [translator of Tappo], Geo Nichol [bookseller], were present. After dinner the conversation turned on publications, and it was remarked that the French had presented their distinguished authors to the world in a much more respectable manner than the English had done. Shakespeare was mentioned, and several present said they would give 100 guineas for a fine edition of Shakespeare. Alderman Boydell expressed a desire to undertake it, which was warmly encouraged.'

However, four years later Josiah described it as, 'a work begun in the most prosperous of times and now completing in the most disastrous the arts have ever known'. Work was commissioned from the most celebrated artists in the land. When they began pressing for payment and the promised sales were insufficient, Boydell was forced to use his home as security for loans, including one from his immediate neighbour in Gothic Lodge. The firm was only saved from financial ruin by Josiah's connections. The King gave permission for a lottery to dispose of the paintings, and the cash raised was sufficient to clear most if not all debts.

During the 1840s the house passed into the trusteeship of the Catholic church. The Passionists were a Roman Catholic order introduced to England by Dr (later Cardinal) Wiseman who sent Father Dominic Barberi to view the property.

He found the house perfectly suited, since although not far from London,

> 'it stands in beautiful solitude, where nothing can be seen but trees and sky. The house itself is sufficiently large to contain a good community of the religious, and ... [there] is a handsome large room which can be easily converted into a Chapel. Besides this, the house is surrounded by an extent of good fertile ground, with a garden, a shrubbery and a meadow fit to support two cows, which is a thing indispensably necessary for a religious community in this country.'

According to Fr Dominic, the local residents did not particularly welcome the new occupants who arrived in 1848. He noted, 'the character of coldness which distinguishes the people of this district'. The priests must have made a strong impression on the quiet village, in their distinctive black habits, with a cross and heart shaped white badge inscribed '*Iesus Xpi Passio*.' Furthermore, one of the fathers could not speak any English. There was to be no parish; rather the intention of the Passionists was to hold retreats and set up missions, in particular to help poor Irish immigrants.

The small community numbered four, among them Father Ignatius Spencer, an ancestor of the late Princess Diana. Local Catholic families gave cash and donated items of furniture. The Passionists continued their charitable work and to hold services at West End, but their future was still in the balance. Whether it was the poor

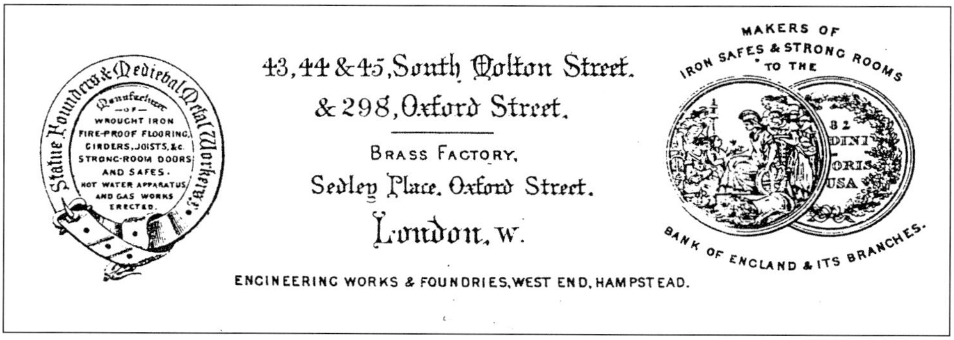

38. Letterhead of Thomas Potter & Sons, ornamental ironworkers, showing their range of expertise and the addresses of their showrooms and factory at West End.

condition of the house, legal difficulties over title, its use as a religious institution or a combination of all three, the decision was made to leave and set up at The Hyde, Kingsbury. The fathers had already opened a centre there, chiefly to help the large numbers of itinerant Irish workers in the area. The move was planned for the autumn, but before it happened Fr. Dominic was unexpectedly taken ill, and died on 27 August, 1849.

Poplar House stood empty and shuttered for a year. In 1851 Thomas Potter moved into the mansion and the property remained in his family's hands for the next forty years. A typical example of the new gentry class whose money came from trade, Potter was an ornamental iron founder with premises at 44 South Molton Street, off Oxford Street.

Examples of the firm's work are hard to trace. The railings of the Royal Courts of Justice in the Strand and several fine brass lecterns are ascribed to Potter, as is the delicate grille work used on the front elevation of St Pancras Station. The company also secured what must surely have been the contract of a lifetime, to renovate and refurbish Welbeck Abbey for the Duke of Portland. The scale of the contract may have meant Potter needed to expand to fulfil its taxing requirements. By 1861 he had built a foundry in his back garden, roughly on the site of the present Welbeck Mansions in Inglewood Road. He could certainly afford it – bills show that over £130,000 was paid to the firm between 1869 and 1877 when the Abbey work was still ongoing! Potter used some of the money to purchase property adjacent to Poplar House, ending up with an estate that took in all the land up to Mill Lane, round to what later became Sumatra and Inglewood Roads.

One of his many purchases was a house that stood on the corner with Mill Lane, facing the village Green. The tenant in 1800 was Samuel Brawne. The family did not stay long, but on 6 August a child was born in the old house. Baptised in Hampstead parish church and named after her mother, Frances or Fanny was to gain fame through her love affair with the poet John Keats. According to Keats,

> 'Fanny was beautiful and elegant, graceful ... fashionable and strange... She is about my height – with a fine style of countenance of the lengthen'd sort – she wants sentiment in every feature – she manages to make her hair look well – her nostrils are fine – though a little painful – her mouth is bad and good – her Profile is better than her full face which indeed is not full but pale and thin without showing any bone.'

An affectionate if unsentimental picture.

It is tempting to hope there could be some link between the Brawnes' brief sojourn at West End and the poet Leigh Hunt's equally short stay in the village some years later. However it appears pure coincidence – he was recovering from a debilitating illness when in 1812 he rented what the rate books describe as a house, coach-house and stable, a little south of the Brawne mansion. Hunt wrote to a friend about his new home.

> 'I am only now gaining strength by slow degrees and small portions of exercise .. I shall get, however, into the country, though scarcely out of town - being about to move, as I believe I told you, to a cottage at West-end Hampstead, where I do not despair of seeing you sit down with me to a plain joint and pudding,

39. *West End House, a watercolour by Emslie, showing the main gates on West End Lane and on the left, the niche well in the wall.*

some day on your return. The cottage is really a *bona fide* cottage with most humble ceilings and unsophisticated staircases; but there is green about it and a little garden with laurel: and I can put you in a room where there will be a little library of poets, and an original portrait of Milton to overlook us as we sit drinking our glass of wine – so that you shall not help enjoying yourself in some measure... The lane to West-end runs out of Kilburn a little beyond the turnpike. My cottage stands in the heart of the place [and] on the gate my name in a fair plate of brass.'

NEW WEST END HOUSE

Across the Green and facing the gates of Poplar House was 'an old roomy brick mansion' said to date from the late seventeenth century. In the eyes of many West Enders, this had the best claim to be the village's own 'Manor House', while the Miles family who occupied it for the best part of the nineteenth century were regarded by many as unofficial lords of the manor. Its grounds reached as far east as Finchley Road and south to meet those of Treherne Lodge.

Some historians have confused this house with the mansion south of the village owned by the Beckford family, as both were referred to as 'West End House.' The locals appear to have used the relative ages of the buildings to distinguish between the two, calling Beckford's property 'Old West End House' and the house by the village green 'New' or simply 'West End House'. Then in the 1890s the name was briefly changed to West End Hall.

In December 1800 Mrs Walpole, the tenant of West End House, entertained a passing troupe of merry carol singers one of whom described the events of the night:

> 'Last night on the rounds with a carolling party. We started at nine with lanterns, a merry group. Called at many houses, Upper Flask House, Branch Hill Lodge, West End House, and then to North End. Much humour and sport and as much mulled ale as we could carry. At West End the Honble. Mrs Walpole gave us a supper of steak pie and brawn. We were home by three o'clock this morning.'

The Miles family moved to West End House in 1814. Born in Liverpool in 1784, John came to London to work for his great uncle, the publisher Joseph Johnson, inheriting a half share in the business on Joseph's death. He met and married Ann Chater in 1810. The house was progressively enlarged to provide space for their growing family – 11 children, born between 1811 and 1830.

The family took an active interest in local events and politics. John lined up with Germain Lavie to oppose West End Fair, as well as serving on parish committees to examine the Poor Rate and monitor the extension of Hampstead Parish Church, where the couple are buried. The family even provided a limited 'speaking clock' for the village, when few of the cottages would have had access to their own timepiece. Locals recall a night watchman patrolling their grounds and calling out the hour 'in slow bass notes, something after this style – past ten o'clock, star light night'. Other more practical help was given to

40. (Left) John Miles, the book publisher, who lived at West End House from 1814 to his death in 1856.

41. Four generations of the Miles family. Seated from left to right we have Mrs Ann Miles's son Joseph Johnson; Mrs Ann Miles; John Miles, Joseph's son. Lying in front is Ann's great grandson, John Marshall Miles.

the villagers: establishing Emmanuel school, while Ann set up coal, clothing and blanket clubs as well as a savings bank:'it was quite an annual event to see the villagers trooping to Hampstead to buy their winter clothing'. In the days before the welfare state such charitable handouts were all that was available. Ann later became a keen supporter of the Temperance movement and went so far as to provide a coffee stall, presumably to try and lure villagers away from the local pubs.

Despite the considerable age of some of the houses, only one ghost story has been discovered for West End and concerns the Miles property – not the house but the grounds. A woman in old-fashioned clothes was said to appear by gates guarding a rear entrance, near the junction of Finchley Road and West End Lane. Headless, she walked down the carriageway rustling her silk skirts, the victim of some dreadful injustice at the hands of a previous owner. Paranormal considerations aside, this entrance was only created after Finchley Road opened in 1829, so what was she doing here at all, by gates erected long after her demise? But maybe the story provided inspiration for Wilkie Collins when he wrote *The Woman in White*, and described his hero meeting a ghostly figure near the Miles property, where four roads join: 'the road to Hampstead, along which I had returned, the road to Finchley; the road to West End and the road back to London'.

John Miles died in 1856 but Ann remained in her old home until she succumbed to a stroke just a few months short of her 99th birthday in 1889. Their son, Charles Miles, trained as an architect but died young, aged just 33. Perhaps the most idiosyncratic member of the family was John and Ann's grandson Eustace Hamilton Miles. An outstanding athlete, among his many sporting achievements he could list several years as amateur champion of England, the US and the World at racquets and tennis. He taught sport and wrote widely on this subject as well as religion, history and aids to learning. But Eustace's passion was diet – the British Library catalogue lists nearly 80 books under his name on the subject. He followed a strict vegetarian regime and opened the 'Eustace Miles Restaurants' in London, to try and convert the public to his tastes. Unfortunately they were often the butt of jokes – 'the place where people who look like garden pests eat like garden pests'.

Mrs Miles' daughter Anne commemorated her mother's long life at West End by donating a drinking fountain to be placed in the centre of the Green. This was recently restored to working order by Camden Council and is now listed. The cattle trough which formed the second part of her gift has long since disappeared.

WOODBINE COTTAGE

The 46 acres of West End Farm bordered Finchley Road, extending to and beyond Fortune Green. In 1755 the property was bought by Henry Flitcroft, its ownership descending through his family until the land was sold for development. Flitcroft was an eminent architect (he built the church of St Giles-in-the-Fields) who lived up the hill in Frognal. His son was declared insane, and his illness may have led to the farm being neglected; in 1805 all the buildings were in poor condition, with the bill for repairs estimated at £250. Perhaps in an attempt to bolster income from the property, a new house was built on the southern edge of the yard. Rented to a series of well to do tenants and known as Woodbine Cottage or Lodge, it was 'a delightful little Regency villa with plaster walls painted white and iron verandas painted apple green', having a garden in front and behind, plus a coach house and stable formed from part of a barn.

In 1853 new tenants appeared for both the farm and the villa. This complex of buildings was among the most secluded in the village, a fact which may have decided William Eley to lease Woodbine Cottage. He was co-owner of Eleys the cartridge makers and he part built, part converted some of the outbuildings into a factory. The locals reputedly refused to work there, perhaps because the firm's reputation preceded it. In 1841 William's father had been killed, 'blown to atoms by fulminating powder' in his Bond Street factory. The firm's sketchy archive records a move from Charlotte Street to Bond Street, then to Broad Street, Golden Square (1851), and finally to the Old Welsh School premises in Gray's Inn Road (1857), but makes no mention of West End. It may have been the intention to make percussive caps there, but perhaps the 'factory' became more of a research facility, which would explain why no locals were employed. The villagers were however only too happy to take part in target practice at the regular shooting parties held in the grounds of the villa.

William and his mother moved to West End from Golden Square after the new 'factory' had been completed. In 1854 a dreadful cholera epidemic swept through Soho, their old neighbourhood, and upwards of 500 people died in the short space of ten days. There was no cholera at West End yet that September the disease killed poor Mrs Eley. Her niece who had been visiting also died. The mystery was solved when Dr John Snow found out that Mrs Eley had a bottle of the Broad Street pump water sent to her new home every day, as she liked the flavour! Sad though it was, the circumstance of her death was so singular that it helped prove once and for all that cholera was a water-borne disease. Fortunately, William did not share his mother's tastes, otherwise the Eleys' stay at West End would have been over very quickly. William was succeeded at Woodbine Cottage by his brother Charles.

The reputation of the last occupant of Woodbine Cottage may also have preceded her, as she had not only spent much of her early life in the public eye but also arrived in the wake of a scandal. Laura Eliza Jane Seymour Thistlethwayte went from highly paid courtesan to respectable married lady in the space of just a few years. Born plain Laura Bell in Newry, Co. Down, she came to London in 1850 and by the time she was twenty, it was said she already had several wealthy lovers, among them Prince Louis Napoleon, Lord Hertford and Prince Jung Bahdoor, the Nepalese Ambassador. It was rumoured that the Ambassador had told Laura that if she ever needed help, she should send him a ring he'd given her as a sign. So when the Indian Mutiny broke out in 1857, Laura is supposed to have contacted the India Office who sent both the ring and a letter from her to the Prince, requesting Nepal remain neutral or support England. The Prince chose the latter.

An admirer described Laura as;

> 'Pretty, with a doll-like face, her big eyes, not ignorant of an artistic touch that added a lustre to their natural brilliancy, and her quick vivacious glances as she sat in her open phaeton, vivaciously talking with a variety of men, all 'swells' of the period, of course, at the corner of the drive near the Achilles Statue (in Hyde Park). She was the talk of the town, her beauty celebrated in popular ballads – Laura, Laura, We adore her!'

However spectacular, Laura's 'career' was a short one. In 1852 she surprised polite society by marrying Captain Augustus Frederick Thistlethwayte in the fashionable church of St George, Hanover Square. His father was a wealthy Hampshire landowner, who had been MP for the county and his mother was the daughter of the Bishop of Norwich. On the face of it, not a marriage made in heaven. Cynics said the main attraction of the otherwise unexciting Captain was his considerable income: 'she induced a foolish person with a large fortune to marry her'. While the couple's problems became public knowledge, there is no firm evidence to suggest Laura was unfaithful. Outwardly, she embraced her new life with enthusiasm and even went a step further down the path of repentance. She got religion, starting by distributing pamphlets to shop girls with evangelical zeal and then going on to hold prayer meetings in her comfortable home at 15 Grosvenor Square, and lecturing to packed audiences at the Regent Street Polytechnic.

Perhaps her most distinguished if controversial visitor at Grosvenor Square was the Prime Minister, Lord Gladstone who had the dangerous habit of befriending 'fallen women'. They met on one of Laura's regular rides in nearby Hyde Park, and he became a close friend and confidant, reading Laura's autobiography, which sadly has not survived. It was even said Laura knew of Gladstone's resignation in 1892 before the Queen did. In his letters he called her Mrs T. The true nature of their relationship will never be known although there was certainly a strong element of physical infatuation on his part. *Vanity Fair* went so far as to write, 'Mr Gladstone has been her faithful disciple, sitting at her feet and cutting up her meat'. His wife was not introduced to Laura until 1887.

The Thistlethwayte marriage ended as it had begun, in scandal and speculation. Augustus kept a revolver by his bedside and would occasionally fire it at the ceiling to summon a servant. On the night of 7 August, 1887, the household was roused at the sound of a gunshot. Finding the door to their master's bedchamber locked, the staff forced an entry and there was Augustus, dead in bed, with a bullet through his skull. The inquest recorded a verdict of accidental death rather than suicide. The will revealed that aside from a couple of small bequests, the Captain had left his entire estate of over £71,000 to his wife. Laura decided to make a new life for herself elsewhere.

The couple already had a country home at West End – Augustus had taken a lease on

42. View of West End Green, showing the Miles fountain and Alexandra Mansions. When West End Green was earmarked for development local people formed a Defence Committee. In 1882 the fence enclosing the Green was burned down by a group of protesters supported by a crowd of about 2,000 people. Eventually, after much negotiation, the Vestry purchased the land for public use in 1885.

Woodbine Cottage in 1880. It was an obvious haven for Laura. She continued to devote her time to good works, contributing to local charities and the work of nearby Emmanuel Church. She saw to it that the Woodbine Cottage gardens were improved, with flower beds planted so thickly that no earth could be seen, the resulting pattern resembling a Brussels carpet. Perhaps to discourage any sightseers curious about her past, a large notice appeared in the grounds facing Cannon Hill with the chilling words 'Trespassers, Beware of Man-Traps and Spring Guns'. It seems unlikely however that such unpleasant devices were ever put in place. One old resident recalled how as a boy he used to trespass quite safely in her grounds 'in search of acorns and adventure'. Moreover, Laura was also an ardent supporter of the Society for the Prevention of Cruelty to Animals and had a number of deer which were allowed to roam freely through the grounds.

Gladstone continued to visit Laura at her new home, albeit infrequently, his arrival a matter of great interest and pride to the locals:

> 'He arrived in a one horse brougham and his face looked very pale, statuesque and serious. My brother and I respectfully raised our hats as the great man was driven through the gates, but he took not the slightest notice.'

However it seems likely her repeated demands for attention became a nuisance; in 1883 Gladstone wrote, 'she has cooked up a habit of much fuss about small things'. He destroyed the letters Laura wrote him, but she kept his, which were recovered by Gladstone's family after she died. Laura did not however attempt to embarrass him by publicising their friendship and even left him out of her will. She died at Woodbine Lodge in May 1894. Her obituaries made lengthy mention of her religious fervour but her past was not mentioned and is buried along with the lady, at Paddington Cemetery. There is a certain irony in the fact that she lies in the Thistlethwayte family vault, beside her mother in law, the Bishop's daughter.

CHOLMLEY LODGE

Cholmley Lodge stood across Fortune Green Lane from the village farm and Woodbine Cottage. It was one of West End's youngest mansions, dating from 1813. Henry Smith Bigg bought the house in the 1830s. He was responsible for enlarging

43. Cholmley Lodge, the last remaining 'gentry' mansion in West End.

and improving the Lodge at a cost of £1,000, and added the portico over the main entrance, probably to Charles Miles' plans. Bigg sold the house to his tenant Herbert Norman Evans, who kept it for upwards of 23 years.

The next long-term occupant was Captain Henry Wilkes Notman, under whose hand the estate assumed its final form, taking in all the land currently covered by Cholmley Mansions. Notman was Managing Director of the South Indian Railway and Secretary of the Salisbury and Yeovil Railway Company. Born in Aberdeen he was a great supporter of Scottish charities and institutions, and nicknamed the 'father' of the Caledonian Society. In common with so many of the other gentry, Notman also helped out local causes, with the largest single contribution – £100 – to the fighting fund to preserve West End Green and £350 towards building the new Emmanuel Church.

BURGESS PROPERTY

The last mansion was a long way beyond Cholmley Lodge, right on the boundary with Hendon parish. It too was a recent building, unusual in that it only ever belonged to the family which built it. The house stood on a low hill roughly where Burgess Hill is today, with sweeping views across open countryside towards Wembley and Harrow.

In the late 1820s the area was too remote to attract speculative development but at the same time it had the definite advantage of the Finchley Road and access to London. Perhaps this is what attracted Henry Weech Burgess who bought the fields in 1838 and proceeded to build his house. The family came from Tiverton in Devon. Henry perpetuated the old field names and called his home 'Temple Park', after the Knights Templar who in medieval times owned the land around. He later enlarged the estate, by buying a triangular field that formed the junction of Finchley and Fortune Green Roads. In 1862 Henry tried speculating, building six houses in the style of the large stuccoed Belsize Park properties on a short length of road that was later to become Burgess Hill. Eventually he even decided to abandon the mansion he had so recently created.

Westward Ho!

The major transformation of Kilburn and West End into suburban neighbourhoods occurred over twenty or thirty years, at the end of the nineteenth century. The willingness or ability of owners to sell their land in favourable economic conditions were most important in this, and the influence of London's building booms and troughs also made their mark. Public transport might support or could even be used to promote new building, but on its own it was never the sole reason for development. But the deep scars made by the several rail lines that crossed the district were another matter. They had a definite effect by dictating road patterns.

A small spate of speculations on the Hampstead side of the Edgware Road in the 1820s was followed by a period of inactivity that lasted into the 1850s and 60s when the first large scale building plans got underway on both sides of the main road. The '70s saw growth where building had already started or been planned. But the '80s witnessed an explosion of building activity which carried over into the next decade, until little open space remained.

During the nineteenth century the great majority of housing was built on 'spec' – tenants were found as building continued or after the house was standing – so if the builder misread the market and over-extended he faced major financial problems. Land owners or builders did not just build the houses – they were responsible for the infrastructure of their own developments, including the construction of roads and most of the sewers.

By the turn of the century, the outer suburban frontier could be firmly placed at Childs Hill, across to Cricklewood and south Willesden. New forms of housing appeared, notably mansion flats, but terraces still predominated. New neighbourhoods emerged: West End was superseded by West Hampstead while Brondesbury and Mapesbury took their names from the old estates in the area. Local retail centres were created, while new churches and schools took care of the residents' spiritual and educational needs.

A special feature of these neighbourhoods was the large contribution made by Land Companies, particularly the United. They tended to purchase smaller properties, subdividing them into plots sold at a series of auction sales, which could mean many builders were involved in the final development. A number of astute business men also emerged. They acted as middlemen, buying up large properties and selling them on at a profit. This meant that several of the old owners failed to realise the best price for their property.

The large houses were sold off to speculative builders, slowly at first, and then in a rush during the 1890s. But it comes as something of a surprise to find that some owners held out, proving that it was still possible for old values to co-exist with suburbia lapping against their brick walls, well into the next century. And it became apparent that unless something was done quickly, all the fields would disappear under bricks and mortar. One solution was for the Vestry to try and buy some of the remaining land for use as public open spaces. West End Green and Fortune Green were saved, but where the campaigners tried to buy an estate that had been earmarked for building, they lost out to the developer, with the single exception of The Grange.

AWAKENINGS

In 1819 Fulke Greville Howard, the new owner of the Abbey Farm Estate at the bottom of Kilburn, let two sites for building, bordering West End Lane and Maida Vale. George Pocock laid out plots in Greville Place, as well as along the main road, just south of the Kilburn tollgate. It was a bold enterprise. For many years Greville Place remained a cul-de-sac, a finger of housing reaching into open fields, intended to appeal to a wealthy class of tenant. The villas along the Edgware Road were christened Kilburn Priory. Despite early high expectations – 'this was certainly one of the best speculations he ever made' – the plots were slow to let. The collapse of a building boom post-1825 and the high interest he owed on loans, all but broke Pocock. He ended up in debt, an inmate of the King's Bench prison in Southwark and the first of the neighbourhood's many speculative builders who faced bankruptcy. George Pocock died at his Kilburn home in October 1829.

The land let by Fulke Greville Howard on West End Lane was also a failure for the two speculators, Henry Jay and John Gelsthorp. Howard failed to stipulate the value of the houses to be built and the result was Abbey Lane, a narrow entry lined with small cottages. By 1825 both developers had been declared bankrupt but

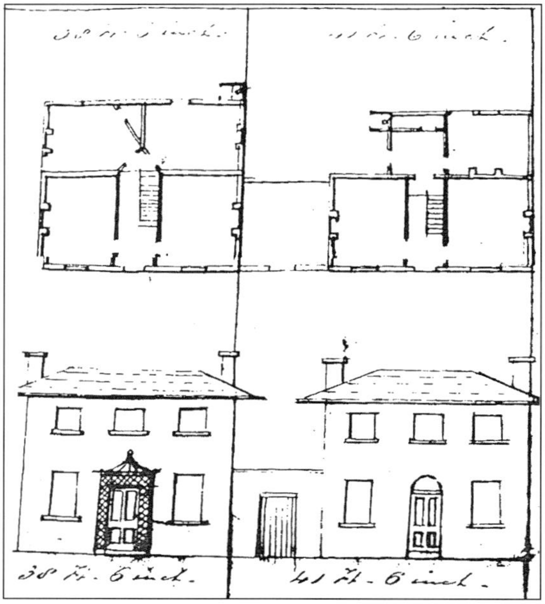

44. Drawing of two cottages in Abbey Lane, off Belsize Road, since demolished and replaced by the Kilburn Vale estate.

45. A view of St Augustine's Church, looking up Rudolph Road from Carlton Vale.

growing demand for cheap housing meant that the few cottages they had built were always occupied.

The area was still predominantly rural – John Pocock's diary recalls many walks along fieldpaths to Willesden and St John's Wood. He and other children made good use of their country playground, from Guy Fawkes celebrations in 1826 when 'a sham battle was very well kept up by the boys who divided into two companies on either side of the Kil-bourne and assailed each other with squibs, and crackers', to sliding on the frozen brook or bathing in a field pond on the road to Willesden and visiting the nearby Bell Tea Gardens 'where we took some cyder'.

ON THE WILLESDEN SIDE

The earliest development on the Willesden side dates from 1850 when the Rev. Edward Stuart sold 47 acres to a consortium of five builders who were responsible from 1851 for laying out the Kilburn Park Estate, beginning with Cambridge, Malvern and Pembroke (later called Granville) Roads, They then subdivided and sold off the remaining lots. However, like many other speculators they eventually became bankrupt. The first houses were built in the ambitious style of St John's Wood, but potential homeowners were put off by the isolation and the unmade and

increasingly muddy roads. As late as 1887 most of the planned houses remained unbuilt.

Lady Salusbury, who owned the Manor and Brondesbury estates, sold her properties to the Church Commissioners in 1856 and from 1857 the Commissioners made a series of agreements with James Bailey, a builder from Maida Vale, who later moved to Brondesbury Lodge. His first houses were laid out on the Elm Lodge estate. In 1859 he had built Brondesbury Terrace and started work in Canterbury Road. By 1867 he had put up about 550 houses using architectural pattern books.

The 1860s marked a turning point for the neighbourhood. As part of a general upturn in building during the latter part of the decade, pockets of housing broke out like a rash across the fields of West End and Kilburn. These early developments were conspicuous for the amount of property sold to Land Companies.

Kilburn Manor House survived until about 1860 when Oxford and Cambridge Roads were laid out. After it had been pulled down one writer remembered the house in its former glory:

> The Manor House, Kilburn, with its lovely old trees and antique gables, formed a pretty picture, which many of the locals felt should never have been destroyed. It stood on the summit of slowly rising fields, near a footway [now Cambridge Road] leading to the Harrow Road. Some beautiful views of the house were obtained from the path.

Local builders began on Brondesbury Road and Villas north of the London &North Western Railway line in the 1860s while Kilburn Square, part of which existed by 1851, was laid out. The fourteen acres of the Victoria Rifle Ground were sold for building in 1866. Two years later the Church Commissioners began granting building leases on the Mapesbury estate.

THE EFFECT OF RAILWAYS

On the Hampstead side the first plans were made by the owners of Old West End House estate. Together with their neighbours, the Ripleys, they were the hardest hit by rail expansion. The Hampstead Junction separated much of the rear garden from the old mansion, which was clearly no longer a high-class let. The last 'gentry' tenant, Daniel Whittle Harvey, left in 1857. The new owners appear to have been a consortium of speculators with the wonderful names of Bischoff, Bompas and Coxe. But what about the house? Fortunately the little matter of a railway crossing the back garden had no effect on a group of

46. Oil painting of West End by G.A. Storey, 1858, looking across the fields towards Kilburn.

47. Old West End House, which in 1858 became a Servants' Training School with a matron and 40 young female boarders.

Trustees, looking for suitable premises to open a Girls' Laundry and Training Institution for Young Servants. However worthy the cause, it was hard work for the poor girls, who were bluntly described as:

> 'Especially liable to fall into temptation [due to] the degradation of their relatives or their own peculiar characters. It must not be supposed that the inmates are trained merely to be laundry maids as they will be carefully instructed in housework, needlework and plain cooking, to establish the principle of training girls to earn their own maintenance.'

In 1863 the Midland line to St Pancras was sanctioned, its route lying right through the centre of the remaining Old West End House fields. Running in a deep cutting it altered the landscape forever and left few options to the owners. They sold three newly completed villas to the rail company who used one as a station building. The Midland also rented and eventually purchased the old mansion after the Laundry School moved on.

In 1864 Donald Nicoll, the owner of the Oaklands Hall estate, let a long narrow plot off Kilburn High Road to Elisha Bannister, a local builder. Palmerston Road was the result and like the Abbey Lane experience some years earlier, it seems that little control was exercised over what was finally built. Within a few years the road was known as a slum neighbourhood.

The Powell Cotton family was also busy, making a start by developing fields adjacent to Abbey Farm, using an old farm track over the Kilbourne stream, to give the line of Quex Road, followed by Birchington and Mutrix Roads in quick succession.

The speculators were also active on land owned by the Ripley family north of Palmerston Road. In 1869 Thomas Tyndale Ripley sold the property to the British Land Company, which kept the larger plot north of the Hampstead Junction Railway and disposed of the six acres south of the tracks to another Land Company, the United. Here the classic combination of neglect and multiple occupation meant Netherwood, Kelson and Linstead Streets gained a similar reputation to adjacent Palmerston Road. In 1881 a Mr F. Holmes was summonsed for non payment of

48. *A very early photograph taken from The Elms on Kilburn High Road, looking across the fields towards Abbey Road. Behind the row of houses is the bridge over the Kilbourne before the construction of Quex Road. This is the only photograph of the river in the area that is known to exist.*

49. Early photograph of Kilburn High Road looking south, showing Muncey's dairy. Most of the site was later taken for the B.B. Evans store.

rates due on the twenty houses he owned in Netherwood Street. A bookseller who had bought the properties as a speculation, Holmes was unable to get the money from his tenants. He had asked the Vestry to visit the area as it was in dire poverty. One poor woman had already been sent to the workhouse, but she said she would rather die than be separated from her child. Mr Holmes added that she was dying now.

The British Land Company managed a slightly more spacious layout for their roads, which they called Iverson, Maygrove, Loveridge and Ariel. Many of the houses were named either as part of a terrace or individually, a respectable step above their neighbours across the railway embankment.

In West End, Cannon Hill replaced an old footpath while across the village green Thomas Potter put up West Cottages to provide homes for the labourers in his nearby foundry. He had found it necessary to import quite a number of skilled workers and with them came their wives and children. The villagers were supposedly hostile to the incomers, refusing them lodgings. This may be true but space was in any case at a premium in the village, as no new cottages had been built for years.

An article which appeared in *The Builder* magazine in 1870 described the character of the area around and south of West End, and pinpointed with remarkable accuracy the nature of changes to come.

> 'The landscape, fieldwards, is studded with the residences of the wealthy (but) looking across the valley in the direction of Kilburn, stakes are driven into the earth, marking the outline of future 'roads,' 'avenues' 'terraces' and so on.
>
> Pursuing our way homewards down West-end-lane, we find they have not begun to move much there yet; but after crossing the two railway bridges (carrying the Midland and the Hampstead Junction lines), we come upon the outpost works of advancing London.
>
> 'Where will London end?' we said to a respectable-looking man who was surveying the situation, like ourselves and with a very suspicious brick and mortary appearance. 'Goodness knows,' was his reply. 'Building plots are snapped up as if they were so many gold nuggets. You go today and all but settle; only you think that you'll consider for a day or two. By the time that you have made up your mind some 'early bird' has dropped down at the land agents and gobbled up the morsels that you had set your heart upon'.
>
> Resuming our walk we came upon Oaklands Hall: the house will be soon surrounded and beleaguered by the restless guerrilla villa, detached and semi detached. The owner, if he would be alone, must betake himself to the distant wilds of some unknown, indiscoverable country where the trowel of the bricklayer is never heard.'

And as history showed, this is precisely what happened.

THE VICTORIAN SUBURB

West End certainly saw more changes in the 1870s. After providing accommodation for railway navvies building the Midland Line, Old West End House was emptied and demolished. The railway proved an effective barrier, the area to the north remaining very much a village, still a country neighbourhood. West End Farm lost twenty acres as the site for Hampstead's new municipal cemetery north of Fortune Green and the West Middlesex Water Company built a reservoir at the Shoot Up Hill end of Mill Lane.

Thomas Potter made a tentative start on his fields off Mill Lane which he christened the 'West

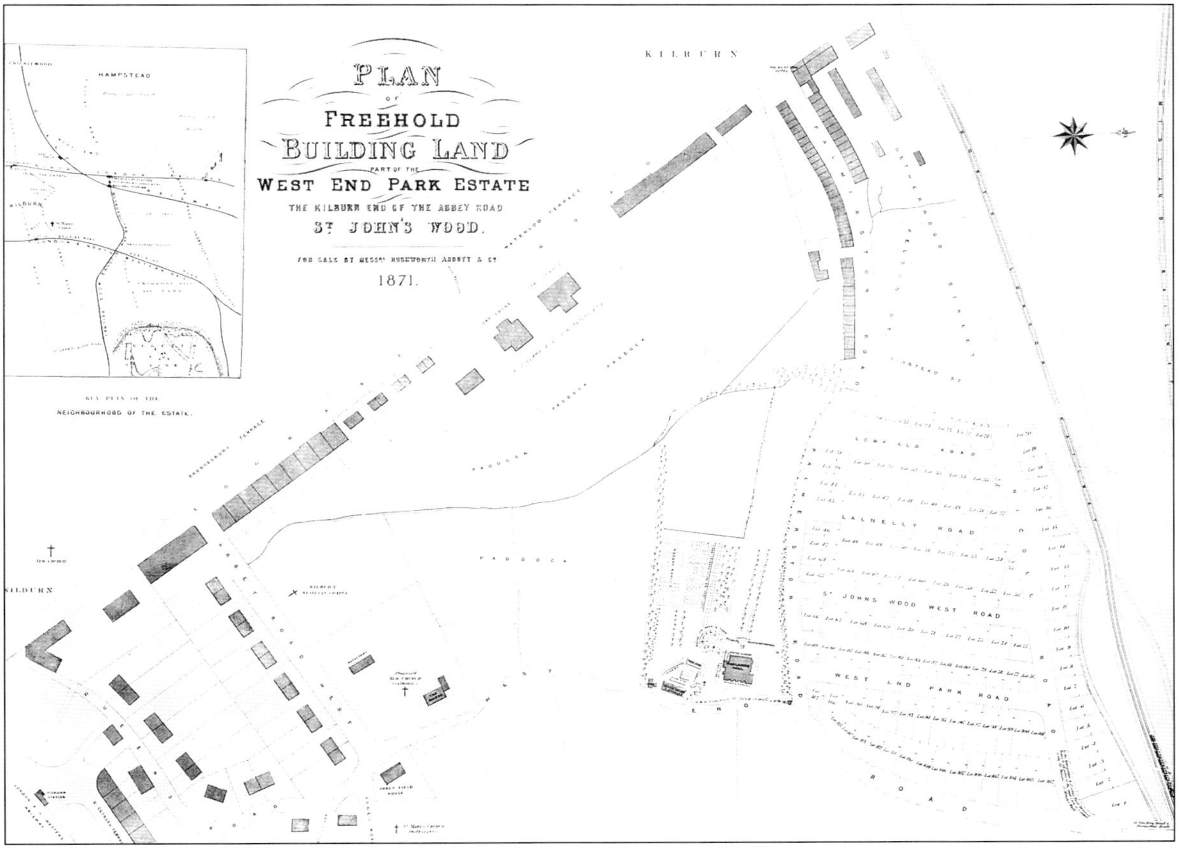

50. Sale plan of West End Park, 1871. This was a speculative development by Donald Nicoll, north of Oaklnds Hall. The final form differed from the plan and is now covered by roads between Hemstal and Sherriff Roads.

End Estate', laying out Narcissus Road. Field Lane Industrial School now occupied a large site on the north side of Hillfield Road while the first Emmanuel Church at the corner of Aldred Road and Mill Lane opened its doors in January 1875 with seating for 120 people. The seventies saw a welcome extension of mains drainage in West End although many of the old cottages near the Green and on Mill Lane were overcrowded and in need of repair.

Across Kilburn High Road 52 acres of the Brondesbury Estate were offered for sale in 1879. The author George Eliot, who lived by the Regent's Canal in St John's Wood, wrote:

> 'I go out every day, drive beyond the ranks of hideous houses on the Kilburn outskirts and get to lanes where I can walk in perfect privacy among the fields and budding hedgerows.'

As an example of the rapid expansion in the London suburbs, Baker and Sons announced in their annual report for 1880 that they had sold 482 acres of land for building at a total of £225,216. This covered property in Hampstead, Willesden and elsewhere. But the major transformation of the area was still to come. In West Hampstead, the 1881 population of some 8,000 had grown to nearly 30,000 by 1901 and house numbers had risen from around 900 to the 3,500 mark. Some of the them were occupied by second or maybe even third generation Hampstead families, but an enormous number of newcomers moved into this and other similarly fast growing districts. In Kilburn, the number of houses rose from 2,000 in 1881 to 3,600 by 1891.

The combined Oak Lodge and Lausanne Cottage estate in Kilburn was sold in 1876 to Jacob Francis Hirsch and eventually acquired by the

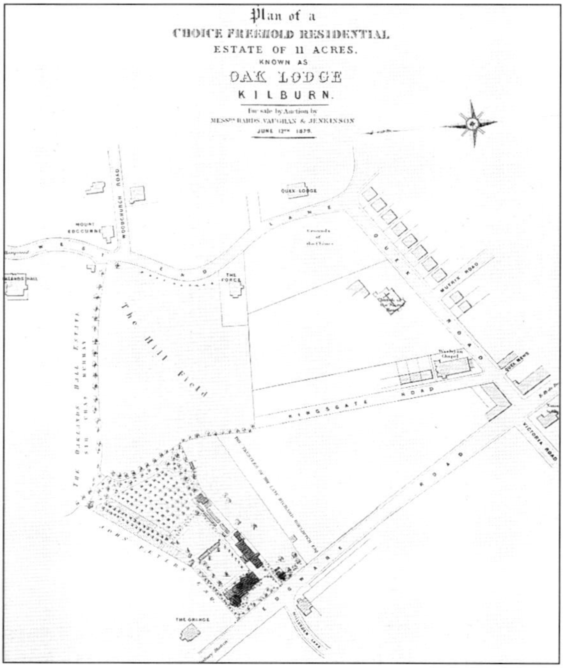

United Land Company. They also bought the neighbouring Oaklands Hall estate which was auctioned off in building plots in March and April 1883 at the Victoria Tavern on the corner of Willesden Lane. The total sum reached over £24,000. The houses built on these plots today make up Dynham, Cotleigh, Hemstal, part of Kingsgate and part of West End Lane.

Across Kilburn High Road, the whole of the Church Commissioners' estate, east of Salusbury Road and south of the London & North Western line, had been built by 1887. To the north of the railway line the streets were laid out as far as Victoria Road and building was complete on the Elm Lodge Estate. The United Land Company bought part of the Kilburn House estate in 1869 and the rest in 1882 and 1883, after John Farmer had left the house. Kilburn House was demolished in 1882, when Glengall Road and Priory Park Road were built. By 1890 the streets

51. Oak Lodge Estate sale plan, 1878.

52. The first West Hampstead library, built in Westbere Road. It was destroyed by a bomb in the Second World War.

53. Shoot Up Hill, looking north from the corner of Exeter Road.

stretched westwards to Paddington Cemetery. The area immediately south of the Hampstead Junction railway line saw no major building until the late 1880s despite the fact that in 1858 the Church Commissioners had leased the land to the Kilburn Brewery with permission to build houses.

Building on the large Shoot Up Hill estate belonging to the Powell Cottons also began. Further perpetuating the family's Kentish roots, Fordwych, Garlinge, Minster, Richborough, Sarre, St Cuthbert's and Westbere Roads were all started in the 1880s.

In West End, Thomas Ripley sold his Little Dene property to Charles Paine in 1882. He kept the mansion and built Dennington Park Road in front of the old house. Kingdon and Pandora Roads plus a short length of Holmdale completed the estate.

Thomas Potter continued work on his 'West End Estate', adding Solent, Glenbrook and Sumatra to existing Narcissus Road. The roads by Fortune Green, Achilles, Agamemnon, Ajax, Ulysses and Gondar were begun by 1886, while across Fortune Green Road, a start had been made on Weech, Burrard, Ingham and Parsifal Roads.

54. Looking north up Fortune Green Road, c.1906.

55. Buckingham Mansions on West End Lane, some of the many new mansion flats.

56. The low buildings and chimneys on the left formed part of the Lodge house which originally guarded the entrance to Sandwell House. In this view of 1963 a row of small shops has been built on to the front. It survived until the redevelopment of the block in the 1980s.

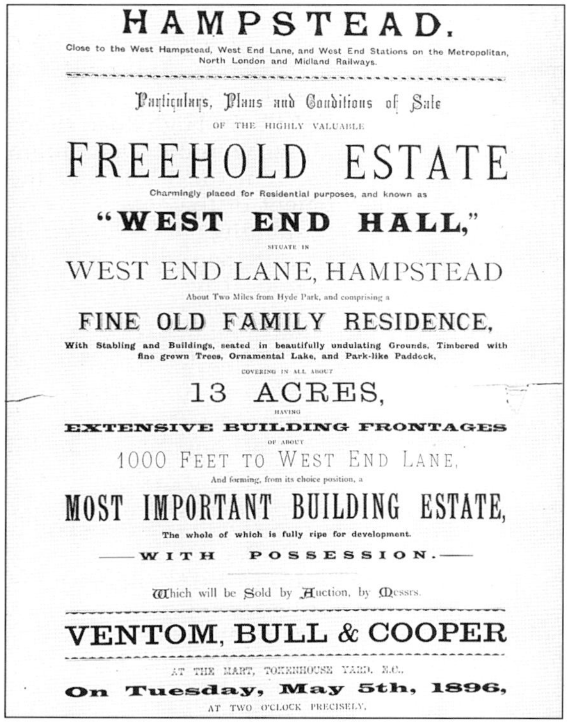

HAMPSTEAD.

Close to the West Hampstead, West End Lane, and West End Stations on the Metropolitan, North London and Midland Railways.

Particulars, Plans and Conditions of Sale

OF THE HIGHLY VALUABLE

FREEHOLD ESTATE

Charmingly placed for Residential purposes, and known as

"WEST END HALL,"

SITUATE IN

WEST END LANE, HAMPSTEAD

About Two Miles from Hyde Park, and comprising a

FINE OLD FAMILY RESIDENCE,

With Stabling and Buildings, seated in beautifully undulating Grounds, Timbered with fine grown Trees, Ornamental Lake, and Park-like Paddock,

COVERING IN ALL ABOUT

13 ACRES,

HAVING

EXTENSIVE BUILDING FRONTAGES

OF ABOUT

1000 FEET TO WEST END LANE,

And forming, from its choice position, a

MOST IMPORTANT BUILDING ESTATE,

The whole of which is fully ripe for development.

—WITH POSSESSION.—

Which will be Sold by Auction, by Messrs.

VENTOM, BULL & COOPER

AT THE MART, TOKENHOUSE YARD, E.C.,

On Tuesday, May 5th, 1896,

AT TWO O'CLOCK PRECISELY.

57. The 1896 sale of New West End House (Hall), the home of the Miles family for 75 years..

An observer noted in 1886 that during the past three years over 800 houses had been built: 'the transformation of 'West-end' which was nothing but a quiet rustic nook, into 'West Hampstead' possessing hundreds of residences, is one of the most remarkable changes to be found in any London suburb'.

As the 1880s drew to a close there was a keen sense that the entire neighbourhood and more especially the old village of West End was witnessing the end of one way of life and the beginning of another. This went so far as to include its name, as 'West Hampstead' increasingly took over from 'West End.' Some claimed to have helped the process along. Thomas Bate, a local estate agent and property developer, wrote to the Metropolitan Railway who approved his suggestion that their new station on West End Lane, opened in 1879, should be called 'West Hampstead.' The change certainly seems to gain momentum from late 1870s and was a logical choice, helping to avoid confusion between the Hampstead suburb and the 'West End' residential and retail area of London around Park Lane and Oxford Street, but the ancient name continued in sporadic use into the next century.

The 1890s saw nearly all the remaining open space disappear. They were also notable for the emergence of the mansion flat. Though the English preferred to live in houses, a block of flats had the advantage of maximising the use of a relatively small and enclosed plot. And mansion flats were also seen as a way of living in a better neighbourhood than you could otherwise afford. But some flats were large enough to accommodate at least one live-in servant and they often had communal and well maintained gardens. Whole street frontages were now given over to this form of housing – notably along Honeybourne Road, and the land enclosed by Lyncroft Gardens, Cannon Hill, West End Lane and Finchley Road.

On West End Lane, Lauriston Lodge was sold in 1891, and the site used to build Hampstead Synagogue and a row of shops. Sandwell House survived until 1897, standing immediately behind Sandwell Mansions.

New West End House, Treherne and Canterbury Houses were all sold to a developer who laid out four streets – Crediton, Fawley, Honeybourne and Lymington. Shops were built along the prime West End Lane frontage.

Mrs Thistlethwayte, the owner of Woodbine Cottage, died in 1894. The property was sold to a group of local speculators who demolished the villa and built Lyncroft Gardens across its grounds, selling a corner plot as the site for a new Emmanuel Church, which moved there from Aldred Road.

THE FINAL PHASE

The new century saw only a few of the old mansion houses still standing. Amazingly, St Margaret's was destined to outlive them all, hemmed in behind the Kilburn High Road shops and adapted out of all recognition. Demolition of the building dates from the 1970s and the Sainsbury redevelopment of the entire site.

The Elms was still standing in 1893 next to 'Palmerstone Works' which then occupied all the grounds. About 1910, local historian Stanley Ball said: 'The house still stands, but is converted into offices by Mess. John Allen and Sons, the house is hidden by shops extending northwards from The Terrace'. This was Allen's building works, Elm Yard, in Kilburn High Road. The end came in 1937, when the house and the small shops which fronted the High Road were demolished and replaced by the State Cinema.

Nearby Mapesbury House in Willesden Lane continued to be used as a horse training centre by Charles Foulsham up to 1916, although the estate around it was filled in with houses. The house was demolished in 1925.

Brondesbury House, having remained empty for some time, was leased as a school to Margaret Clark from 1882 to 1898 and then to Lucy Soulsby from 1898 to 1915. It continued as a school until 1934 when it was described as 'shabby-looking' and was finally bought by C.W.B. Simmonds, a builder, who pulled it down to make way for Manor House Drive.

In West Hampstead, the Burgess mansion disappeared under the triangle of Burgess Hill, Ranulf and Ardwick Roads. Cholmley Lodge survived the longest. A resident wrote a letter to the local newspaper in 1909.

> 'Sir, I think it will interest nature lovers and your readers generally to know that on Tuesday afternoon a cuckoo sang lustily in the beautiful grounds of Cholmley Lodge. It seems somewhat remarkable as the grounds are closely surrounded by houses.'

As was the case elsewhere in the neighbourhood, the house had survived because of the long life enjoyed by its owner, Captain Notman, who died in 1914. The estate was put up for sale and in 1922 the Council approved plans for the first of the many blocks of flats on the site. Cholmley Lodge was demolished in 1925.

58. West End Lane looking north from the corner of Compayne Gardens.

Redevelopment and Renewal

DEALING WITH SLUMS

It took a long while before effective legislation was put in place to remedy poor housing . Local authorities lacked powers to demolish and redevelop areas of old or neglected properties until the 1890 Housing of the Working Classes Act enabled them to build and own houses. And after 1900, councils could buy land outside their boundaries for housing purposes. But they were often reluctant to act, relying instead on their public health departments to enforce repairs on individual properties. More recently, pressure to find sites was increased through the introduction of laws obliging Councils to extend the option of municipal housing to a far wider cross section of the population.

Housing conditions in parts of Kilburn were particularly bad. In December 1881 a public meeting was held in Kilburn Town Hall to discuss conditions in Victoria Place behind the Cock Tavern. Only men over 21 years of age were admitted to the meeting because of the shocking nature of the disclosures! It was revealed that 161 people, 44 men, 33 women and 84 children were living in 26 small dwellings. There was only one entrance, a covered way, from the High Road next to the pub's urinal where the walls were covered in bad language. A committee was formed which included Thomas Bate and George Kalber, the proprietor of the Cock, to persuade the landlords to build a new entrance and brick up the old one. But whether this subsequently happened is not clear.

In 1898, the Vestry investigated living conditions among some of their most under-privileged residents, living in Palmerston Road and Kelson and Netherwood Streets off Kilburn High Road. The majority of the houses were registered as 'houses let in lodgings' and the Medical Officer of Health reported:

> 'No case of actual want or destitution came under my notice, while the children looked healthy, well fed and fairly clothed. It is possible that parents and young children sleep, eat and wash in one room. Provided that the cubic air space is sufficient, your Vestry, as the Sanitary Authority, has no power to intervene'.

Many of the residents kept hens:

> 'It was stated that the birds afforded a valuable reserve of animal food in the winter when men were out of work. In the interior of the houses the chief requirements were the need of cleansing, whitewashing etc of ceilings, and the repair of the plastering of the walls, which were frequently destroyed by the young children. The total number of souls in the 160 houses was 2264, of which 668 were children under 10 years of age, an average of a little more than 14 for each house, against 7 for the rest of the Parish'.

But there were also a number of old properties in the old village of West End, some dating from the eighteenth century, that attracted a great deal of adverse comment. Essentially these were rural cottages which later became part of a suburb.

Providence Place, a group of cottages near West End Green, was often brought to the attention of the authorities. Improvements were made to their general sanitation, but essentially these were 'add ons' and never wholly satisfactory. Unscrupulous landlords also subdivided the houses as a simple way of providing more accommodation and higher rental income.

In West End 13 new cottages for workmen were built from 1863 onwards by Thomas Potter. They faced an open ditch that was unhealthy and smelt foul, especially in hot weather. His tenants said that while the cottages were in 'an open locality, and well adapted for working men's families, containing every requisite for health and cleanliness, the doctor was almost a daily attendant upon their children'.

Off Kilburn High Road, several small streets clustered south of the London North Western line were also cramped and insanitary. There was an open sewer in Goldsmiths Place and reference was made to the 'abominable basements of the houses, Manchester Mews was in an untidy and filthy state in 1863, being badly paved, badly cleansed and apparently a common receptacle for rubbish'.

The new houses in Abbey Lane and Kilburn Vale built from the 1820s had many problems. 'Mud Alley' was the local name for Abbey Lane for many years. In 1866 a few houses were described as 'in a most foul, unwholesome state, and should be pulled down, or at least made fit for human beings'.

In 1905 Hampstead Council attempted to deal

with Kilburn Vale but as the London County Council refused to implement the 1890 Act or contribute to any scheme, Hampstead could only refer the 66 houses, home to 318 people, to the Council's Public Health Committee. It took two years to prepare a report that came to the obvious but not very helpful conclusion that the area was in a 'very unsatisfactory condition'.

In 1920 Kilburn Vale was yet again described as 'a collection of very old houses badly arranged, close and confined in their general condition and lacking proper conveniences and containing sanitary defects that can only be effectually dealt with by a reconstruction scheme'.

A beginning was made on slum clearance by Willesden in 1938 when houses in Alpha Place, off Canterbury Road were pulled down. Surveys of the Church Commissioners' estates in 1944 and 1948 showed that south Kilburn was grossly overcrowded and dilapidated.

REDEVELOPMENT

There were a number of private redevelopment schemes between the wars, many of them in the form of flats. To find room for these, Victorian houses with large gardens were demolished, particularly on the old Powell Cotton estate where the early development had been more spacious. The houses on Shoot Up Hill between Minster Road and Garlinge Road were targetted by developers and by 1939, eight of them had been replaced by over 130 flats. The large houses between West End Lane and Priory Road, Powell Cotton territory again, were also fertile ground for conversions, as were the even more substantial properties off Kilburn Priory.

The inter-war years were also notable for the first large-scale municipal housing. As there were no suitable sites within the borough, Hampstead Council in 1933 bought the 18.5 acres of Westcroft Farm, conveniently located just over its boundary in the borough of Hendon. It was estimated the site could provide around 290 homes of varying sizes. The suggested rents varied from 9 shillings a week for a one bedroom flat to 15 shillings for a four bedroom house, and 21 pram and cycle sheds were provided. At the end of October 1935, the Westcroft Estate was officially opened by the Duke of Kent. 'His Royal Highness expressed surprise that a housing scheme on such a scale was needed for Hampstead, until it was explained to him that the many mews in the district created a problem of a special kind'. His secretary later wrote to Hampstead Council forwarding the gold key which was presented to him when he opened the Westcroft Housing Estate, 'intimating that His Royal Highness would like the present and any future tenants of No. 11, Howard Close to keep the key as a memento of his visit'. It would be interesting to know if it is still in their possession.

THE EFFECTS OF WAR

World War I had relatively little impact on the district –Zeppelin raids were infrequent and casualties from air raids were few. Some bombs fell near Belsize Road and one in Oxford Road in January 1918 and in the last raid on London in May 1918, a bomb fell on the railway sidings in Canterbury Road.

A visitor to Greville Place that night recalled that he persuaded a cab driver to:

> 'venture on the long drive to Kilburn in the blackout which was enshrouding the whole of London. Later that evening the maroons [air raid warnings] went off announcing an air raid. Bombs began to burst in rapid succession. To judge from the violence of their explosion they were dropping none too far away. Anti-air-raid guns had come into action; shrapnel from our barrage was dropping about the house, which stood in its own grounds with a glass dome over the hall, the panes of which were shaking. The air raid was a nerve-racking, noisy affair, stretched over hours. When at last the 'all-clear' had sounded it was immediately followed by another air-raid warning, as a single enemy raider was still caught within our barrage. It was long, very long after midnight when I left Kilburn on my dark walk back to the Ritz.
>
> I had to find my way round the first bomb crater at the corner of Greville Place and the Edgware Road. There was much similar damage and destruction upon the whole upper reaches of the Edgware Road. Willesden Junction it was believed, had been one of the German targets.'

A search of the 'Soldiers Who Died' database shows that 491 soldiers who died in World War I were born in Kilburn, and another 41 were born in West Hampstead.

In October 1914 the local newspaper celebrated the 'Kilburn VC Hero'. This was Battery Sergeant Major George Dorrell, of Kilburn Park Road.

59. World War One Special Constables. The group includes Sir Francis Hayden Green, who lived in Inglewood House, the flats on the corner of Inglewood Road.

With two other members of his battery he won the award at Mons for sticking to his guns.

Though West Hampstead and Kilburn received some bombing in the Second World War, it was relatively light considering the area's important complex of railway lines. Across Hampstead, 200 people died and 407 houses were destroyed with damage to a further 13,000 properties.

The first local damage occurred in September 1940, in and around the Kilburn High Road, as bombs fell on the Brent side. Later, eleven policemen were killed when Salusbury Road police station was destroyed. 1944 was one of the worst years. In February three incidents occurred on one night. In the first, a bomb destroyed part of a parade of shops on the corner of Dennington Park Road and West End Lane, including the shop previously owned by the Cross family.

> 'In a flat over a butcher's shop a party was in progress attended by relatives and friends of the occupier's son who was to be married later that day. The company remained during the alert in unprotected rooms, no doubt lulled into a false sense of security by the long period of aerial inactivity. A high explosive bomb fell at ten minutes past one in the morning, demolishing the upper part of the premises over the shop. Many attempts were made to reach the victims by working upwards from the basement but difficulties were encountered with fire and falling debris. The premises were soon burning furiously. The only survivor from this party of eleven men, women and children who had remained behind was the father of the bridegroom who had left the room and gone to the rear of the house (local rumour has it to visit an outside toilet) just before the bomb fell. The dead included two small babies'.

In other incidents nearby, 16 people were killed in and around Agamemnon Road, and a mother and baby died in Buckingham Mansions. The first of the dreaded 'flying bombs' (the V1) fell in the early hours of a morning in mid June, at the back of 42 West End Lane. This house, which was being used as a refugee hostel, stood roughly opposite Gascony Avenue.

60. A World War II tank outside Finchley Road tube station

> 'Three houses were destroyed; the damage was so widespread it affected at least five roads, and extended over a quarter of a mile. Carlton Mansions was seriously damaged. Four persons were rescued alive within the first two hours. The casualties were eight dead; fifteen missing; and 68 taken to rest centres. With the aid of the Fire Brigade who kept the debris damp with water from the hoses, the rescue work continued for two days. At the end of the first 24 hours, seven of the fifteen missing were found – killed outright by the explosion. Two others died in hospital. A woman was rescued alive after 48 hours. This new bomb came over night and day, spluttering its way to bring death and destruction to the homes of ordinary people living in quiet streets'.

A second V1 fell in Ardwick Road damaging houses there and in neighbouring Finchley Road and Burgess Hill, another in the garden of North Hall, Mortimer Crescent and a fourth destroyed houses in Fortune Green Road. In mid August a flying bomb fell on the Willesden side of Shoot Up Hill, variously reported as killing ten or thirteen people.

Then in January 1945 the first V2 rocket in the area exploded on the railway embankment in Iverson Road and caused substantial damage. Three people were killed and well over a hundred injured. A driver of one of the first rescue vehicles had the dreadful experience of finding his daughter aged 19 was one of the victims, killed by falling masonry. The damage spread over a wide area: over two hundred houses were seriously affected and fourteen completely destroyed in Sherriff, Maygrove, Ariel, Loveridge, Iverson, Lowfield Roads, Netherwood Street and on West End Lane. A further 1,678 other houses sustained some minor damage, some as far away as Broomsleigh and Ravenshaw Streets. The next rocket fell in Willesden, by the railway embankment in Dartmouth Road. It caused severe property damage in and around Fordwych Road where 175 houses were affected but no loss of life in Hampstead.

A less important but unusual casualty of the Second World War in Kilburn was a record breaking car. George Eyston, while on holiday in Le Mans in 1921, decided he wanted to become a racing driver. During the next few years 'The Captain', as he was known, began to win races driving a range of cars such as Aston Martin, Bugatti, Alfa Romeo and MG. In 1936 his car, *The Speed of the Wind*, captured the world record at 162 miles per hour. Then in a new car, *Thunderbolt*, he competed against John Cobb and by 1938 he had raised the record to 357 mph. In one of the flying bomb attacks during WW II *the Speed of the Wind* was destroyed at his Kilburn workshop, but Eyston was not hurt.

POST WAR DEVELOPMENT

It was obvious that demolition and rebuilding were the only options for some of the worst damaged property. Bombed areas provided the Councils with the best opportunity ever to provide new municipal housing. But temporary housing was also needed for the homeless and returning soldiers and their families. Unoccupied houses and flats were taken over and short-term homes provided. In March 1946:

> 'Local residents seeing workmen busily engaged in erecting a hut-like structure on a bombed site at the corner of Dennington Park Road, this week, stopped and stared: 'The first prefab house in Hampstead?' they asked one another. But it isn't. It is being erected to serve as offices for the War Damage

Commission who, under pressure from the housing authorities, are moving out of No. 10 Dennington Park Road to make room for homeless families'.

The largest area of prefabs (single storey houses made of prefabricated panels) was built alongside the railway line in Westbere Road, 84 in all. Although intended as a stop-gap solution, they were finally demolished only a few years ago.

In the 1950s, new Council blocks were built on bomb sites in West End Lane (Sidney Boyd Court), at the corner of Dennington Park Road (Dennington Park Mansions), on Fortune Green Road (Walter Northcott House), on Shoot Up Hill (Templar House) and in Burgess Hill (Mackellar House).

In the new post war spirit of optimism, such schemes were regarded as major milestones and the opening ceremonies seen as important events. The Council invited the Princess Royal to open Templar House, for example.

But the problem of the old run-down areas off Kilburn High Road persisted, now joined by others in the neighbourhood, where housing conditions were fast deteriorating. Kilburn Vale and Kilburn Priory neighbourhoods were tackled soon after the end of the War. The Vale occupants were rehoused in other LCC estates early in 1947, but only three families, who could prove long links to the neighbourhood, were relocated in Hampstead. The Kilburn Priory area was redeveloped as flats in the Kilburn Gate estate.

As part of a redevelopment plan for South Kilburn, Willesden Council bought 61 acres and began building on the bombed sites in 1949. In the 1950s and 1960s a further 59 acres were acquired. The first stage of the plan was completed by 1964 when the church and houses of Kilburn Square were replaced with a shopping precinct and 17-storey tower blocks.

Around Palmerston Road the Webheath scheme made specific provision for low-level housing in parallel blocks running east-west. While the road pattern was retained, the demolition of houses in Palmerston Road and Netherwood, Linstead and Kelson Streets followed. Work began in 1968 with the first stage ready for occupation in August 1970. At the foundation stone laying ceremony, Dame Florence Cayford, one of six Labour councillors who had gained control of Kilburn ward in 1930, was interviewed by the local press.

'When we were first elected, some of the older councillors didn't even know where Kilburn was. The houses were in poor condition. They needed bathrooms, proper sinks and toilets. They could have had them if the old Hampstead council had taken an interest. Another trouble was inadequate drainage. The sewers and pipes in the area hadn't been renewed for years, and when there was a heavy thunderstorm, you knew there

61. Kilburn Bridge, looking north up the Kilburn High Road, showing 1960s redevelopment in South Kilburn.

62. Kilburn Square, a 1960s redevelopment which included a two-level shopping precinct. This has recently been modified to include a permanent market.

was going to be flooding on Kilburn and parts of West Hampstead. Basements were always being flooded. The slime used to get up to the mantelpieces in some places'.

A large area off Kingsgate Road was tackled next. In 1967 it was claimed 8,170 residents would be displaced of whom 7,200 would be rehoused in 'up-to-the-minute conditions'. The redevelopment of the large area between Kingsgate Road and the High Road was undertaken by Camden as part of the Kingsgate Environmental Area. Unfortunately, the final scheme was but a shadow of the original planning brief. A baths/leisure complex which included two squash courts, two exercise rooms, laundry facilities, hot baths and showers, with possibly a playground alongside were planned for a site near the Quex Road junction, but failed to materialise. Meanwhile across Quex Road, between it and Mutrix Road, most houses were demolished and replaced by another low-rise development, opposite the 1950s flats of Kilburn Vale.

In 1972 a local newspaper noted that 41 West End Lane was shortly to be demolished to make way for the Council redevelopment. The house had been the home for many years of the Friday family, which had apparently worked with radium before they were obliged to emigrate to England during the last war. In this house Mrs Friday and her family established the Radium Light Company, which painted luminous dials on instruments. The work was carried out in the house, probably in the basement, where the radium compound was stored after delivery in small phials embedded in lead balls. Concerns were raised about the levels of radiation in the house. The article concluded that although the levels were probably too high for living accommodation, they were 'almost certainly not harmful' – indeed, in the context of a factory they were acceptable. Reputedly the bricks of the house were removed and buried twenty feet deep in a GLC dump.

63. Children playing in a boarded-up doorway of a South Kilburn street, prior to its demolition.

More recent Camden schemes have been a new estate on the Council depot in Lymington Road, and off Iverson Road the West End Sidings estate was completed on redundant railway land. A third estate replaced the old 1950s prefabs in Westcroft Road.

Working Lives

TILE MAKING

There are records of tile making in Kilburn in the 16th century. Parish documents note that in 1570 Richard Laye, a Tylemaker of Kilburn, was buried in Willesden churchyard. In his will he left money, cows, wheat, and rye to his wife and children. A tilehouse in Kilburn was listed as part of a disputed property in 1600. Intriguingly, Ben Jonson, in his last complete comedy, *A Tale of a Tub* (1633), included a character called the 'Tilemaker from Kilburn', suggesting that it was a well-known area for tile production.

William Freelove is named as a tilemaster of Kilburn in the 1650s. The tilekiln on the Liddell estate had become a private house by 1698. There was a Tilekiln house on the Roberts estate at Kilburn in the 16th century and this was probably 'The Place, tilehouses and kilns' on the Edgware Road which were sold by Thomas Roberts to Thomas Marsh in 1679. This, together with Tile Kiln farm or Kilburn Pitts, was owned by the Marsh family in the mid-18th century. The kiln had probably stopped working by the late 18th century when the farm was merged in the Salusbury estate.

The only reference to tiles on the 1762 Hampstead estate map is a six-acre field named as, 'Tile Kiln Field alias Great Pitts now divide into two'. This was part of Liddell's farm, which lay to the west of West End Lane and was occupied by John Pollett. On the Willesden side a 1765 Terrier shows two fields named as 'Kiln Fields', occupied by Joseph Gibson. They are just south-west of Brands House in Mapes Lane. In the 1815 Terrier they are called 'Little Kiln Field' (21 acres) and 'Great Kiln Field' (37 acres), and were part of the Brondesbury estate, occupied by Paul Giblett. With the rapid building development in the area tilemaking was replaced by the need for vast numbers of brick. Brickmakers were noted in Kilburn in 1851 and in 1867.

AGRICULTURE

There were six farms on the Hampstead side of Edgware Road, some with local farmhouses and yards. On the Willesden side farms were part of the three large estates of Bounds (Kilburn Manor House), Brands (Brondesbury) and Mapesbury. The Kilburn Bridge farm, of about 40 acres at the bottom end of Kilburn, lay in the parish of Paddington. As all the woodland had been cleared by the mid-eighteenth century and arable had given way to grass, by 1814 it was said that Hampstead's farming was dependent on supplying hay to the London market. Quite a few wealthy local residents were also butchers, like Charles Spain at York Villa, or coachmasters and stable owners, all of whom needed fodder for their horses or beef cattle. The fields were also used for grazing dairy cattle and short stay stock, using manure to keep them fertile. The Westminster Dairy Company (*see p.30*) rented land off Edgware Road for a while in the 1820s.

Because Hampstead's farming was not labour intensive, few families made a living from the land. In 1801, of the 412 men, women and children resident in Kilburn and West End, only 45 or 11% worked on the land, and of these a number were gardeners. At harvest time any shortfall in the local supply of labourers was made up by travelling bands of workers who slept, as they laboured, in the open fields. The actual numbers employed at the various farmhouse complexes remained low; in 1851 William Baker, lessee of 290 acres of land, employed only six full-time labourers and in 1871, Charles Roach had just one man and one boy helping him on West End Farm.

The hay crop continued to be worth harvesting, with opportunities exploited whenever possible. In 1875 Hampstead Cemetery contracted with local West End farmer John Cotching who agreed to pay £1 a week for the land before burials got underway.

Kilburn Mill on top of Shoot Up Hill, which ground corn, employed a small number of men and operated for a hundred years.

Kilburn Nursery, occupying the triangular plot where the High Road and Kilburn Priory meet, was run by a French family named Goubert. The business lasted until the turn of the century. In 1881, Jean Goubert employed 23 men and nine boys. The family also had Brondesbury Nursery at 67 Kilburn High Road on the Willesden side in 1894. Other nursery gardens included Chambers at West End Green, who later moved up the road to Fortune Green. The Henderson family who ran the Pine Apple Nursery in Maida Vale, also had the nursery adjoining the grounds of The Grange.

64. Goubert's Nursery near Kilburn Bridge showing a 'Sold' sign, about 1890.

KILBURN BREWERY

In 1832 the Verey brothers, William, aged 29 and George, aged 21, obtained the lease of some land and buildings on the Willesden side of the Edgware Road. The property consisted of a house with a paddock, garden and outhouses. The Vereys built Kilburn Brewery on part of the site. The venture proved successful and by 1851 they were employing 22 men. In 1853 they acquired a wharf on the canal at Lower Place, Harlesden, to bring in the malt, hops and yeast they needed. The brewery occupied the stretch between Drake's Yard, where there was a cobblestoned entrance, and Dyne Road. It had a fine frontage, a malt-house and stabling for dray horses and there were two wells for a regular supply of water. The Vereys also ran several off-licences in Kilburn High Road.

William and George, who were born in Bletchingley, Surrey, at first lived next to the brewery at Paddock House, or Paddock Villas. Later George moved to The Elms on the Hampstead side of Shoot Up Hill. After selling the business, George continued to live in Kilburn and in 1881 he was at Holmby Grange on Shoot Up Hill. In 1895 he published a pamphlet with the interesting title, *Suggestions on how to obtain more interest for the Capitalist, more work at better wages for the Operative and Prosperity for all classes*. William died in 1882 in Barnes.

In 1866 the brewery was taken over by Michell and Phillips (which in 1894 became Michell and Aldous). In January 1892 the Kilburn Brewery was almost destroyed by fire, caused by the over-heating of a kiln, but following this it was considerably extended and improved. When it closed in 1920 it employed 66 men. The building was later occupied by the Gas, Light and Coke Co. Several shops are on the site today, including McGovern's pub, but the original facade of the brewery can still be seen above them from numbers 293 to 313 High Road.

SAXBY & FARMER'S SIGNAL WORKS

The signal works in Canterbury Road was the largest employer in Kilburn. The founder of the company, John Saxby, was born in Brighton in 1821, the son of a local dairyman. He became a carpenter and joiner and worked for the London, Brighton & South Coast Railway which began in 1852. In 1856 he took out a patent for his invention of a signal lamp which was linked to the railway points. This was a major advance in safety as previously the points and signals were operated by different people. Now the semaphore signals, the coloured glasses of the signal lamps, and the points could all be activated by means of a single lever. He began to manufacture the new signal gear in Brighton, but in 1862 he resigned from the railway company and joined forces with John Stinson Farmer, to open Saxby and Farmer's factory in Kilburn Lane (later called Canterbury Road), alongside the London & North Western Railway. The Patent Railway Signal Works, as it was called, achieved

65. The Gas Light and Coke Company on the site of Kilburn Brewery, 307-311 Kilburn High Road.

early success when the new stations at Charing Cross and Cannon Street were equipped with their signals between 1864 and 1868. As railways spread across the world the factory grew, so that by 1871 there were 450 employees, and in later years this increased to about 2,000. They provided signalling equipment to Belgium, France, Italy, Spain, Portugal and Russia, and in 1878 opened a factory in Creil in Northern France. In 1881 they constructed the largest signalling apparatus ever made for the Brighton Terminus. Then in 1888, for unknown reasons, the partnership was dissolved. Saxby continued to manage the Creil works until he retired there in 1900 at the age of 79. He returned to England to spend the last years of his life in Hassocks, Sussex until his death in April 1913. The name of Saxby was remembered when the firm was amalgamated with others in 1920 to form the Westinghouse Brake and Saxby Signal Company.

Very little is known about John Farmer, who lived at Kilburn House from 1866 until it was pulled down in 1882. He was born in Shelton, Staffordshire about 1828. The 1881 Census shows him aged 53, living at Kilburn House with his wife Olivia, aged 48 (born in Nottingham), their 17-year-old daughter Emily who was born in Kilburn, and seven servants.

In 1903 manufacture of Westinghouse signals was moved from Kilburn to Chippenham in Wiltshire, where the company still has a factory today. From 1911 to 1933 the site in Canterbury Road was used by the Humber Motorcar Company and then later by Raymond Way, who built up a highly successful car and motorbike sales organisation. No sign of the old Saxby and Farmer building remains and today the site is occupied by a Royal Mail sorting office.

OTHER EMPLOYMENT

During the last part of the 18th and early part of the 19th centuries local employment opportunities were few. The big houses needed only domestic or garden and stable workers, and as we have seen local agriculture did not employ very many people. Some local women took in laundry – there were drying posts on both Fortune and West End Greens – and others looked after 'nurse children'. The annual fair at West End, also gave an opportunity to sell goods and this is why the villagers opposed moves by the gentry to abolish the fair in the early 19th century.

Later, there were new forms of employment in the area.

Potter's foundry near West End Green opened in the 1860s, and although many of the original workers were skilled outsiders there were also unskilled labouring jobs available. Brick making for railway construction and house building was another possibility, and railways and bus services needed many new workers. The 1871 census shows that in West End village occupations were still predominantly manual and unskilled, while those of residents of the new streets off Kilburn High Road included clerks, bricklayers, bus conductors and shop assistants.

Servants were heavily in demand for the larger houses in Kilburn and West Hampstead and adverts gave the wages of a plain cook as '£14 per year, all found, except beer'. A nurse could expect £8. People worked long hours: artisans did 60 hours a week, while shop assistants endured between 75 and 90 hours a week. To reduce the number of hours for the shop workers a public meeting was held at Kilburn Town Hall in 1882 and this led to the introduction of early closing once a week.

In West Hampstead, Sloper's engineering factory, the Tower Royal Works, opened about 1872 in Blackburn Road and lasted until quite recently. The specialities of the firm were woodworking machinery, and perforating machinery for metal, felt and paper.

Work related to agriculture gradually diminished towards the end of the 19th century. There was a veterinary surgeon and forge next to the Cock Inn on the High Road for many years until the motor car replaced the horse. The West End village smithy on Mill Lane closed in 1882. There were still seven slaughterhouses local to shops and houses in Hampstead in 1895, and over the parish boundary in Cricklewood the Dickers' Farm survived until the 1930s.

66. Daintons, builders, at 170 Belsize Road.

Speculators and builders like Thomas Bate, Robert Yerbury and Samuel Dainton employed large numbers of men in Kilburn and West Hampstead. It is interesting to note that all three men came from Somerset.

Of the 238 factories and workshops inspected in the parish of Hampstead in 1898, over 50% were dressmaking concerns. The great majority of residents in the new streets of West Hampstead worked outside the immediate neighbourhood.

From 1916 to 1922 the Central Aircraft Company occupied the Palmerstone Works at 179 Kilburn High Road, the grounds of The Elms. The firm built aircraft parts and produced eight Centaur IV aircraft in 1918 for a flying school it operated at Northolt. Seven other planes were built between 1919 and 1920. From Northolt, which the pilots nicknamed 'Kilburn Aerodrome', the firm gave joy-rides over London in the 1920s.

Other local companies included Beck and Pollitzer, exhibition stand makers who were in Iverson Road, and Cadbury's had a distribution depot off Blackburn Road. Today a major source of employment are the service industries such as restaurants and retail outlets, but most residents commute to work outside.

67. An early photograph of a group of shops on Kilburn High Road, with the Black Lion on the right.

The Traders

Passing trade along Kilburn High Road offered early opportunities for a few enterprising shop keepers, but in West End, where days could go without a single stranger travelling through, only a few shops existed for local custom. Drinking water was sold at a halfpenny a bucket, brought down from Shepherds Well in what is now Fitzjohns Avenue. In 1832, the Kilburn entry in the Middlesex Directory had 33 shopkeepers and traders, including a butcher, fruiterer, baker, two grocers, a cheesemonger and a hairdresser. By 1841 West End still had only a general shop cum beerhouse plus one or two bakers.

In the 1860s a continuous line of shops developed on both sides of Kilburn High Road, but there was no major change at West End. Here one of the bakers doubled as a post office and there was also a letter carrier who took mail to Hampstead.

An 1872 Directory details eight pubs and 108 shops in the Kilburn High Road. The latter included grocers, greengrocers, butchers, bakers, cheesemongers, a fruiterer, fishmonger and a tea dealer. There were also four corn dealers, tailors, hosiers and a linen draper, and three bootmakers. For the growing number of householders, there were builders, carpenters, plumbers, house decorators and painters, a slate merchant, a zinc worker and a chimney sweep. Household goods were available from two ironmongers and the china dealer. On Kilburn Bridge there was a row of eight coal merchants. Services for horses were provided by two wheelwrights, a saddler, farrier and a harness maker. And to hire carriages there was one jobmaster. For the sick there were three chemists and three surgeons (doctors). Other professionals to support the building boom were an auctioneer, a surveyor and a land agent. There was one undertaker and one monumental mason. There was also a commercial photographer. Perhaps surprisingly for such a poor area, there were only two pawnbrokers at the time. There was a confectioner, three tobacconists, three stationers, two hairdressers, two florists, a watchmaker, a fancy repository and a toy dealer. In contrast to today's numerous restaurants and cafés, there was only a coffee room and a dining room. In addition to the eight pubs, there were two beer retailers and two wine and spirit shops.

68. Kilburn High Road south of Willesden Lane looking north. The flags and banners suggest this may have been taken at the time of 'Shops Exhibition Week', a promotion held in May 1909.

69. The decorative shop front of W.H. Smith at 103 Kilburn High Road at the turn of the century.

70. *S.A. Marks, greengrocer at 240 Kilburn High Road, c.1906.*

71. *Kilburn High Road, c.1906, looking south, showing the LNWR station and the Bon Marche.*

THE KILBURN BON MARCHÉ

Founded by William Roper in the 1880s, The Kilburn Bon Marché was for many years the premier business in the High Road. A drapery and furnishing store, it traded at first from a couple of shops south of The Bell. William's wife Stephanie always insisted on being addressed as 'Madame Roper', perhaps because the Kilburn business took its name from a Parisienne shop of the same name. The Ropers lived in Cricklewood House at the junction of Edgware Road and Cricklewood Lane.

On the occasion of their Silver Wedding in 1889, a huge marquee was put up in their extensive back garden, 'providing bathroom, dining room, and side rooms'. The celebrations stretched over three days, and the Ropers inviting their shop staff as well as friends and family. Roper died in May 1891 after a long illness following an accident. As a mark of respect, and a demonstration of the esteem in which he was held, most of the Kilburn businesses shut down for his funeral.

73. Kilburn High Road, near Belsize Road, looking north, c.1906. The bank on the corner is now a health food store.

As was common among drapers' shops at the time, the Bon Marché had 21 'live-in staff' at the time of the 1871 census. The shop was extended and new premises opened in March 1881 when there were 31 assistants living in at 1 and 2 Bell Terrace. In 1882 the Bon Marché announced that they had sold 35,600 Christmas cards. But the same year also saw a burglary when men broke in through the skylight and stole a £200 block of silk cloth.

72. The Kilburn Bon Marche store in Kilburn High Road.

The shop was the scene of probably the first moving picture display in the neighbourhood, a children's display of the bioscope at the cost of threepence a head. Charles Landstone went along.

> 'I, of course, had no idea what we were going to see, though one of my sisters told me it would be like the pantomime. We were ushered down into a small basement at the store; my puzzled mind could only make out a large white cloth which was stretched on the wall facing us, and my sister told me that that was the curtain. I kept asking when it was going to go up, but no one took any notice of me. Eventually to my surprise, the lights went out and moving pictures appeared on the screen. It was all very murky and shaky, and it had no perspective: when figures approached the camera they looked like ghosts. There was a picture of Queen Victoria which was just discernible but it certainly was intriguing.'

B.B. EVANS

Without a doubt, the most famous store in the area was that of B.B. Evans at 142-162 the High Road, a little way north from the Quex Road corner. It was opened in 1897 by Benjamin Beardmore Evans, a Welshman who knew the area well and had served for many years on the Willesden Urban District Council. Over the years his business expanded from a single shop to take over adjoining premises and in 1905 major rebuilding occurred. In 1910 catastrophe struck when the store was gutted by a fire.

So extensive was the damage that an appeal was made for financial help for the shop assistants who lived over the premises:

> So great was the personal loss sustained by some of the assistants employed at the establishment of Messrs. B.B. Evans and Co, drapers, at the time of the destructive fire that occurred there last week, that a fund has been opened at the Church of St Paul for the relief of the distress caused. In certain cases the female assistants have lost almost every item of clothing. Several of the young women are homeless and are being housed in various parts of the parish and neighbourhood.

Despite this setback, the shop rose phoenix-like from the ashes and went from strength to strength, becoming a general department store rather than just a draper's. People would travel to it from miles around, preferring to shop at B.B.

74. B.B. Evans, the major department store on Kilburn High Road.

75. The great fire at B.B. Evans in 1910, which gutted the building.

Evans than go into the West End of London. The founder died in 1915 but business continued. The shop was modernised in 1965 but by now it was no longer independent and in 1971 the parent company decided it had to close. This was the end of the double curved staircase, the palms, the floorwalkers, the whizzing overhead money dispensers, and the clock which was a well known Kilburn landmark. These all disappeared, except for a stained glass window in the reception department of today's Safeway store.

THE GRANGE FURNISHING STORES

If B.B. Evans was the best known shop in Kilburn, then the Grange Furnishing Stores at 127-9 Kilburn High Road on the corner with Victoria Road was certainly its rival as a famous name. It offered a high class of furniture, including the well-known 'G-Plan', and it supplied many of the houses and flats in the area. A 1920 directory shows The Grange Furnishing Stores at 215 Kilburn High Road – opposite the site of the The Grange –and it also had premises on the Victoria Road corner which the 1929 directory calls Trinity House. That site is now occupied by McDonald's, but the name of Trinity House can still be seen above.

CROOK'S, THE UNDERTAKERS

The long established Crook's Undertakers are at the corner of Buckley Road (*see ill. 76*).

Charles William Crook came to Kilburn in the 1850s and set up first as a carpenter and later a job master in Clarence Place, Edgware Road, a group of houses a little way south of the later junction of Eresby Road. The business moved to Quex Mews and Iverson Road, offering a range of vehicles for hire. Four of his grey horses were admired in the Lord Mayor's Show in 1881 when they pulled the Kilburn Volunteer Fire Brigade engine. His brother, James Crook, opened an undertaker's business at 263 Kilburn High Road on the corner of Buckley Road, which is still there today. An advert for the business in 1896 offers 'Estimates for funerals to or from all parts of the Universe'. Until very recently his descendants were still running the business. James Crook was a keen amateur photographer and it is thanks to him that some of the earliest images of Kilburn were recorded.

76. The long-established Crook's Undertakers at the corner of Kilburn High Road and Buckley Road. Note the boy's unusual cycle.

77. Colebrook florists, at 135 Kilburn High Road.

OTHER SHOPS

Colebrook Court Florists, who were at 135 High Road, Kilburn, had held a Royal Patronage Warrant from 1883. When King George V was passing the shop on the way to a ceremony, Queen Mary pointed out the Royal Arms conspicuously displayed over the doorway of the shop. A few days later a court official called to demand their removal because the original recipient of the honour was no longer there. Shortly afterwards, Queen Mary was again in the neighbourhood to open some institution and the presentation bouquet was made by Colebrook's!

William Perring and Co. Furniture Suppliers, 242 and 244 High Road, just north of the Grange Cinema, opened in 1922. The founder was Sir William Perring (1866-1937), a Conservative MP for Paddington. He had opened his first shop in the Harrow Road in 1892 and received his title in 1926 for public service.

Cleaver's Coal, 7 Quex Road. J.D. Cleaver leased the premises in 1891. He became a councillor for the new Kilburn Ward of Hampstead in 1900. When he died in 1921, the business was taken over by his son R.J. Cleaver who also

78. Pegrams grocers, 222 Kilburn High Road.

79. *Waugh and Co, boot and shoe shop, 239 Kilburn High Road.*

80. *Sainsbury's, 292-294 Kilburn High Road. This was their Christmas display.*

became a councillor in 1925. The coal business carried on until fairly recently when the shop became a newsagent's.

Jules Bastling, Court Hairdresser, Artistic Wig Maker and Hair Restorer. 146 High Road, a site later taken over by B.B. Evans. The following advertisement provides a wonderful description of his shop:

> 'Two tastefully arranged windows face the main thoroughfare, presenting a display of attractive specialities; while the contents of the recherché front shop include everything of value in toilet necessaries, perfumery and hairdresser's goods. To the rear is the gentleman's hairdressing saloon, where every modern appliance and the best of machinery is brought into play. Upstairs are two equally complete and comfortable ladies' rooms, one of which is reserved for hair dyeing etc. In the secret of hair dyeing and general restoration Mr Bastling is a master. He guarantees that all dyes used in his establishment are manufactured by himself, of perfectly harmless vegetable matter, no injurious chemicals of any kind being used.'

The *Kilburn Times* newspaper was first published on 14 March 1868, by Rowland George Bassett at 5 Park Place, Charlton Road (Carlton Vale). From 1874 to 1892 it was run by Thomas Smith. The office moved to 175 Charlton Road, and then in December 1871 moved again to 1 Manchester Terrace.

OFF THE MAIN ROADS

The United Land Company set aside shop plots on Kingsgate Road. Charles Landstone, who lived locally, remembers the traders:

> 'The dairies were a Welsh preserve. Our own man Lloyd of 81 Kingsgate Street used to present his customers at Christmas with a splendid cake and much cream: an excellent custom. There was dear old Augustus Schneider who ran a baker's and confectioner's at the corner of Hemstal and Kingsgate Roads. This tall quietly spoken Bavarian had nothing of the harsh Prussian spirit in him but when the first Zeppelin raids came they provided an excuse for an ugly show of mass hysteria and the old fellow's shop was wrecked. Next door to the Schneiders was a general shop run by an elderly French couple, an unmarried brother and sister named Rambeau. They had come to settle here after the debacle of 1870 and setting up of the Third Republic. They were insular and reserved as only the French know how to be and their command of English was limited. The wonder was that they made a living for themselves at all, but they seemed to.'

81. West End Lane, c.1906, with the corner of Sandwell Crescent on the left.

82. Humphrey's dairy at 208 Belsize Road with the delivery boy and his cart.

As a child in the 1930s actor Joss Ackland lived in Hillfield Road, and he described the Mill Lane shops originally known as The Pavement.

'I remember the little row of shops around the corner. The sweet shop with liquorice boot-laces – all different colours; Mickey Mouse toffees – twopence a quarter; packets of Imps – tiny sweets made from liquorice with menthol, with the kick of a mule; penny slabs of chocolate – brown and white; packets of sherbet with liquorice straws; bottles of Tizer and fizzy tablets that exploded in the mouth. There was a chemist that smelt of camphor and a grocer where the salty rashers of bacon blended with the sweet icing smell of biscuit animals, and a hardware store with bundles of wood to light fires and the smell of paraffin lamps, and of course, the newsagent and toy shop with copies of the Buzzer, Magnet, Gem, Champion and Film Fun and many others, sometimes with magnificent free gifts – water pistols, Japanese flowers that erupted from the shells when put in water and divers that bobbed up and down in the bath. And there were the soldiers and the cowboys made of lead – penny ones that stood; twopenny ones on horseback and sixpenny knights with removable swords – mounted magnificent and unobtainable.'

West End Lane and Mill Lane shops were for local residents and had almost no multiples or large businesses that might have drawn custom from outside the area. George Cross moved to the area as a young boy in the late 1890s when his father bought a butcher's shop in West End

83. Mill Lane, looking east; c.1906. The horse and cart are outside the old Alliance pub.

Lane. Business started poorly, but the enterprising Cross family hit on an idea to increase trade – 'why could we not cook and deliver complete with china and cutlery, a hot dinner to every newcomer who would promise to buy our meat?' Over the years this helped takings rise from £50 to £250 a week.

Kilburn attracted large numbers of street traders, whose low prices undoubtedly appealed to some, but many shopkeepers and residents from the better-off streets were anxious to see them removed. The costers counter-attacked with a letter from the long winded if aptly named United London Male and Female Costermongers' and Street Sellers' Benefit and Protection Society requesting that the street sellers be allowed to trade in the High Road on Saturdays, 'half a loaf being better than none'. They were allowed to trade at street corners or in side roads, providing no objections were raised by owners of adjacent business premises. In the 1930s it was suggested

84. Cope Bros., poulterers and fishmongers, 173 West End Lane. This was a promotional card to advertise prices: fresh haddock 7d a pound.

85. Coster cart in Exeter Road.

that St Margaret's or the redundant St Paul's Church be used as covered markets, but it took until 1993 for the Kilburn Square site to be set up. Costers continue to form part of the street scene to this day.

RAYMOND WAY

Raymond Way ran a successful business selling cars. He had a garage on the corner of the High Road and Greville Road, and also premises on the other side of the High Road. The following was written in 1962:

> 'Raymond Way is another super salesman who has made a fortune. Way sells used cars, and has been an extrovert ever since the early days when he rode the Wall of Death. He will sell any car to anyone who can pay for it. To every customer Way gives a cigar in an aluminium tube. In addition to the brand (Jamaican) it bears the message in large red lettering: 'Jolly Good Luck - Raymond Way of Kilburn'. His first deal was twenty-eight years ago. He bought an old car for seven pounds ten shillings and sold it for nineteen pounds. Way realised there was money in this business. He has worked hard at it ever since. Now, at fifty-five, he is a short, slim man with flashing gold in his teeth and lizard-skin shoes on his feet. He looks fit, He is fit. Three mornings a week an ex-army drill sergeant calls at Way's flat (in Mayfair). The sergeant barks orders, Way obeys – press-ups, knee-bends, rowing exercises. A shrewd bargainer himself, he respects the man who tries to beat him down in price. Over lunch one day he told me a story about a man who decided to buy a used car priced at £1,000 and wanted to drive it away. The man offered a cheque in payment. The salesman called Way on the buzzer to get approval for this arrangement. 'Did he try to beat you down on the price?' 'No,' said the salesman. 'Then don't take his cheque,' said Way. He works every day and all day. Much of his business is done on the telephone. If the bell does not keep ringing, he things there must be something wrong. It rarely stops. Raymond Way has little time for books, music or art. 'I don't know how to relax', he says. One thing he does not lack is friends. He is on first-name terms with all the barrow-boys in Kilburn. Many of them have known Way since he started in business there nearly thirty years ago.'

WEST HAMPSTEAD

In West Hampstead a shop owner converted his premises into the first 'self service' store in the early sixties, a tentative experiment with limited stock. At one point West End Lane even supported two record shops, one opened by Shirley

86. The interior of the chemist shop of Alban Atkin at 243 West End Lane, shortly before its conversion into a kebab shop. Currently it is a sushi bar.

87. Williams, fishing rod and tackle manufacturer and umbrella repairer at 256 Kilburn High Road. Note the combination of fish and umbrellas above the shop. In 1891 Thomas Williams (aged 78) was running the shop with his wife, Jane. Mr Williams is sitting on his tricycle.

Bassey. Two of the longest established businesses, Alban Atkin the chemists (no. 243) and Sidney Venning the locksmiths and ironmongers (273), survived until recently. The chemist's shop was a time warp right up to the end, with large glass fronted cabinets and beautiful apothecary jars. The dispensary was at the far end of the shop, under a huge clock but the chemist only made up homeopathic remedies. The window display was a low key one, and for many years its centre piece was a red neon sign draped with a piece of satin and advertising Yardley cosmetics. In Venning's shop, items ranging from watering cans to brooms were suspended precariously from the ceiling. There was a large paraffin tank under the premises and customers queued to have their cans filled. The elder Sidney Venning started the business back in 1915 and Sidney his son joined the business in the thirties. Sidney senior, who died in 1982, was apparently once mistaken for Dr Crippen and arrested at Margate.

The 1980s and 1990s were periods of mixed prosperity for the main shopping parades as well as for smaller neighbourhood centres. Long-term trends such as the number of women who now work and the increase in car ownership, have contributed to changing retail patterns. Custom has shifted to larger purpose-built centres which offer free parking and a variety of stores under one roof. Today fewer people than ever rely solely on local shops and many of them have closed. Restaurants are the current vogue in West End Lane but less numerous on Kilburn High Road. Here some multiples have moved away and the road has failed to maintain the prosperous image of previous decades.

Civic Pride

LOCAL GOVERNMENT

Hampstead and Willesden vestries were the local authorities for West Hampstead and Kilburn until 1900. Their responsibilities included public lighting, but only a small part of Kilburn, near the Bridge, was lit by 1849 and this was not extended until 1861. In 1900 the vestries were succeeded by borough councils which functioned until the creation of London Boroughs in 1965. In that year Hampstead became part of Camden, and Willesden part of Brent.

Hampstead's old administrative centre was the Town Hall on Haverstock Hill, but Willesden's was in Kilburn, in Dyne Road, on the edge of Willesden parish. Willesden Town Hall was opened in November 1891, and was replaced in 1970 by James Stewart House (named after the first chairman of Willesden District Board, who had a draper's shop in Manor Terrace).

Strangely, both Kilburn and West Hampstead had their own 'Town Halls' but these were not local government offices, but privately owned buildings, regularly rented out. They were used for a variety of purposes, from a makeshift mortuary in the case of the 1907 rail accident at West Hampstead Station, to providing regular fund-raising and entertainment venues. Thomas Bate, a local estate agent and property speculator, built Kilburn Town Hall on Belsize Road, a little way south of the High Road. In December 1876 it was reported that:

> 'This spacious and handsome hall is now being patronised by various local and other organisations for lectures, entertainments and public meetings. There is every reason to believe that this speculation of Mr Bate will be a highly successful one. The building has a magnificent concert room, with stage, committee room, ground floor offices, reading room, two large billiard rooms, etc; approx. 4,500 square feet capable of great development.'

Bate was also connected with the establishment of the West Hampstead Town Hall at 165 Broadhurst Gardens, near the junction with West End Lane. He built the 'Falcon Works' on the site but almost as soon as the building was complete he sold it to H.G. Randall, who had a butcher's shop round the corner. It was Randall who converted it into West Hampstead Town

88. Willesden Town Hall, Dyne Road, c.1906.

Hall, starting work as 1886 drew to a close.

> 'Several additions and alterations to the West Hampstead Town Hall have just been completed at great expense. All the cloak-rooms and artistes' dressing rooms have been redecorated, and the large hall, which has a splendidly polished pine floor, has now been well lighted with five large gas stars in addition to a number of tinted lights on the walls. The additions embrace a minor hall, well lighted and warmed, and capable of seating three hundred persons. A capital promenade has been made beneath the main hall, and furnished with garden seats.'

By 1929 it had become a recording studio, and in the 1950s it was owned by Decca:

> 'Strains of the unique sound of Mantovani's orchestra, of the Show Band, of the famous voices of Vera Lynn, Lita Rosa, Joan Regan and Dickie Valentine float over the rooftops of a corner of Kilburn, all day and everyday.'

More recently, the Beatles and Rolling Stones have recorded there but it is now home to the English National Opera. Decca left about 1981, moving to Bate's other speculative venture in Belsize Road, the old Kilburn Town Hall. Surprisingly, the exterior of West Hampstead's Town Hall appears to have survived relatively unscathed.

HEALTH AND WELFARE

In 1875 Mill Lane was suggested as the site for a local hospital, but neither Kilburn or West Hampstead was to have a public hospital of their own – clinics yes, but otherwise residents had to travel to St Mary's Paddington or to New End in Hampstead: 'a child might be sent up to Captain Notman at Cholmley Lodge. You'd pull the bell and hear it ringing through the house, and then someone would come and ask "What is it you want, my dear?" And you'd ask for a letter to take to St Mary's Hospital'. Poor families would pay a 1d a week for each child to make sure of getting a doctor's services.

For many working girls who had unwanted pregnancies, the baby could mean ruin and they often took steps to conceal their condition and gave birth in secret. If they had no friends or relatives to help them or they couldn't afford to 'farm' the baby out, then they would loose their jobs and suffer the stigma of raising an illegitimate child on their own. The following sad report appeared in the local press as late as 1906:

> 'PC 542S, said on Monday at 7pm, he was in the garden of number 18 Birchington-road, for which he was acting as caretaker, when his foot came into contact with something lying close to the wall. He stooped and saw a brown paper parcel, which on examination he found contained the body of a new born male child Dr Henry Robertson, 135 West End-lane, gave evidence showing that the child had been dead twenty-four hours when he saw it on Monday at 7.45pm. Death was due to heart failure from exposure to cold.'

A strange case was reported in 1897, well before the widespread use of domestic refrigerators.

> 'A Refrigerated Baby
> Yesterday evening Dr H.R. Oswald, deputy coroner, held an inquest on the body of a newly-born female child which was found wrapped up in paper in the garden of a house in West-end-lane (number 39).
> Dr J.W. Anderson, of West-end-lane, stated it was a fully developed female child. It had lived probably about twenty four hours, and had been kept for at least six weeks in a refrigerator, or in ice. In reply to the deputy coroner, Dr Anderson would not go farther than to say that death was caused by strangulation probably with a tape or cord. The jury returned a verdict of 'Wilful murder against some person or persons unknown.'

In 1898 the Kilburn Branch of the Social Democratic Federation asked local authorities to consider establishing rate supported hospitals and dispensaries in Kilburn, Willesden and Cricklewood. The Federation was told that while the need was recognised, the authorities had no legal power to use public money for such a scheme. It is hardly surprising to find that one of the first health centres was opened close to the crowded streets off Kilburn High Road.

The Kilburn and West Hampstead Constitutional Club in Kingsgate Road was taken over in 1913 by Thomas Hancock Nunn and reopened as The Hampstead Health Institute, in memory of Edward VII. The adjoining St George's Hall was opened by Mrs Stanley Baldwin on St George's Day, 1929. Nunn's plan to unite vari-

89. The Health Centre in Kingsgate Road.was opened by Mrs Stanley Baldwin, wife of the Prime Minister, in 1929.

ous health facilities under one roof was a new concept in medical care.

ST MONICA'S

St Monica's Home for Sick and Incurable Children opened in 1874 with eight patients and then moved to Quex Road in 1878. By 1901 it had moved again to 16 Brondesbury Park and in 1940 had 26 beds for children of poor parents. It closed as a children's home about 1950 and became a geriatric hospital by 1975.

PUBLIC BATHS

In 1867 the growing number of residents in Hampstead who lacked adequate washing facilities prompted the Medical Officer of Health to recommend the opening of public baths in the Hampstead.

> 'The heat which has prevailed universally during this Summer has brought daily more painfully before me the necessity of Baths and Washhouses in this Parish. In the absence of the former, many thousands of male adults have been driven to bathe in the Heath Ponds, in defiance of a public notice-board of 'Danger and Illegality'. This has been done to such an extent that the stagnant water has become putrid through animal debris. Women and children, however, have been, from sheer modesty, prevented from this resource. '

Probably the residents of Kilburn made similar use of local field ponds, though by 1881 they could use the Kilburn Baths in Goldsmith's Place which were open from 7am to 9pm. But it was the Wells and Campden Trust, a private charity, which first provided baths and washhouses In Hampstead. The poorer streets off Kilburn High Road were seen as the most deprived, and a public baths was opened in Palmerston Road in 1886, containing 14 baths, a laundry and a drying room. The building was later taken over by Hampstead Council. It closed in 1967, its demise hastened by a tremendous explosion which damaged windows on the nearby Webheath Estate and set fire to the roof of the St George's School annexe.

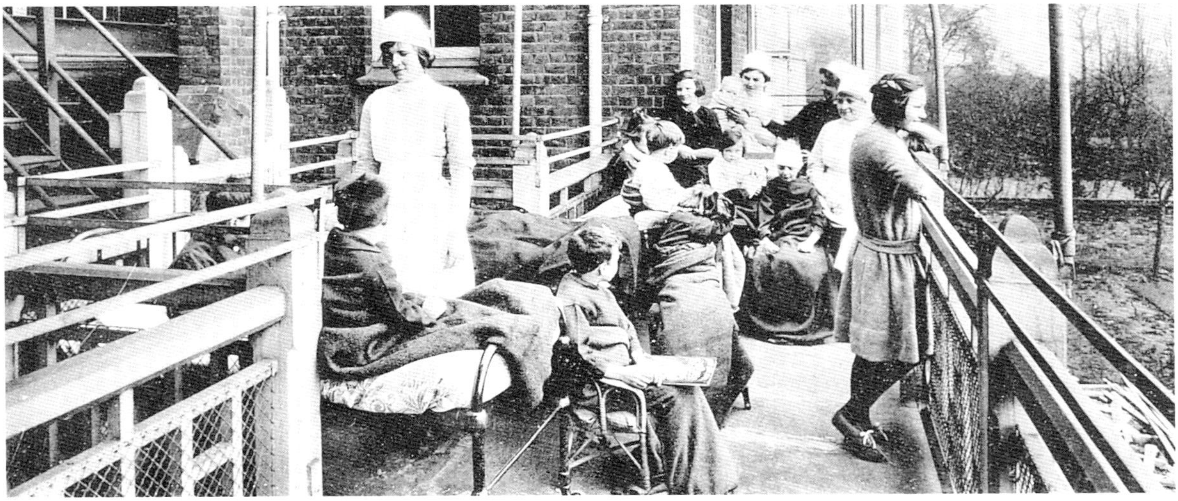

90. Children and staff on the balcony overlooking the garden of St Monica's Home.

91. Brondesbury Park Military Hospital was founded in the First World War by Miss Maude Thomas, Commandant of the St John's Ambulance Association Voluntary Aid Detachment. The house, 'Beversbrook', on Brondesbury Park, was offered by Dr Vaughan.

POOR PUBLIC HEALTH

Dr Thomas, Medical Officer of Health for Willesden, presented his first report at the end of 1875. It painted a depressing picture of overcrowding and disease. There were 1,746 houses with 13,968 inhabitants in the urban portion of Willesden, that is Kilburn. The rest, the rural portion, had only 605 houses with 4,175 people. By 1894 Willesden's total population had grown to 73,640. The Kilburn area was overcrowded with 11 persons per house, compared with six in the rest of the parish.

The Hampstead Medical Officer for Health reported in 1881 that deaths from smallpox were only two for the year. A compulsory vaccination programme was in force against the disease and local authorities worked hard to enforce it against public apathy or opposition. For example, a labourer from Lowfield Road was fined five shillings for not taking his baby to the public vaccinator to check if the vaccination was successful or not after one week. The programme seemed to be working as five years previously 70 cases were reported in the area.

Life was nasty, brutish and short for many people in Victorian Kilburn and West Hampstead. A high death rate of 45 per 1,000 for children under five years old was reported for Willesden in 1875. The worst area was Kilburn, where diarrhoea, tuberculosis and respiratory disease were especially prevalent. In 1912 the county council took control of tuberculosis treatment and established a clinic at Priory Park Road.

Dr Diplock, the coroner for the Western Division of Middlesex, reported that in the year 1880 he had held 695 inquests, of which 293 had been on children under the age of one year.

92. *Hampstead Cemetery and Lodge in 1876, shortly after the cemetery opened. The hills behind are largely a product of artistic licence.*

THE AFTER LIFE

In 1855 Paddington Burial Board established one of the earliest public cemeteries on 24 acres of farm land bordering Willesden Lane, which was part of the Roberts estate. Thomas Little, who had designed the chapel at Nunhead Cemetery, laid out the paths in the shape of a horseshoe. Two entry lodges, and two linked chapels were built. In 1986 Westminster Council sold the Cemetery to Brent.

The parish burial ground at St. John's, Hampstead was proving insufficient to meet the needs of a growing population, so the vestry decided a new cemetery was needed . The Hampstead Burial Board met in April 1873 and after considering several sites, settled on a 20-acre plot adjoining Fortune Green, which they bought for £7,000 in February 1874. After the landscaping and the main buildings were completed the Bishop of London formally consecrated the cemetery in November 1876. The site was extended in 1901 by the purchase of another five acres of land along its northern boundary.

FIRE AND POLICE STATIONS

Following the disastrous fire at the windmill (*see p.14*), Kilburn Volunteer Fire Brigade was set up in December 1863. It was commanded by Captain Mitchell and its headquarters was in Bridge Street, near the tollgate. There was a good engine, but in the event of a fire, the horses had to be brought from a mile away and the volunteer firemen gathered together. The brigade were equipped with a steam engine in 1872 and this quickly proved its worth when it put out another fire at the steam mill that year. In 1881 the *Kilburn Times* wrote in support of the local volunteer brigade and against the proposed take over by the Metropolitan Board of Works. The paper challenged anyone to show such a percentage of quick extinctions of fires. The local brigade, it said, had been at the scene of a fire in five minutes, as against 20 minutes for the Metropolitan Brigade fireman. However, control passed to the Metropolitan Fire Brigade in 1892 and a new station was opened in Salusbury Road in 1894.

As building progressed, alarms were placed at strategic points in neighbourhoods but these were not ideal. In 1889 the LCC considered 'the memorial from the inhabitants of the Kilburn Ward asking for increased protection from fire in that neighbourhood' but decided the area didn't merit its own fire station. Instead it decided to place a fire escape and hose cart in West End Lane and put in eight more alarms parish wide. By 1899 the spread of building made all such arrangements untenable and a permanent solution had to be found and a fire station opened in 1901 opposite West End Green.

The shops immediately north of the station were the scene of an IRA attack in October 1993, when a bomb was placed under a car parked on a pavement forecourt. Fortunately no loss of life

93. The Fire Station opposite West End Green was designed in the style of Voysey by E.E. Brooks of the architects' department of the London County Council. Opened in 1901, it is now a listed building.

94. Kilburn Fire Station in Maida Vale.

resulted, although many nearby windows were shattered by the blast.

Despite repeated incidents of highway robbery of travellers and visitors to Kilburn Wells in the eighteenth century, Kilburn and West Hampstead were poorly served by police constables and watchmen. They were based up the hill in Hampstead village. In 1883 West Hampstead got its own Police Station at 90 West End Lane. In 1891, 15 people were recorded in the building on census night; 6 police constables, plus a sergeant and station inspector and their families. The cells were apparently empty. In 1966 Berridge House, the Domestic Science College on Fortune Green Road, was demolished and the site used for a new Police Station. Considering the bleakness of the building it is surprising to read that it was specially designed to 'blend in' with the surrounding streets and houses! It cost £180,000 and was opened in April 1972.

95. Gipsies on Fortune Green. Gipsies had camped on the Green and nearby Blind Lane for many years. In 1893, when the locals were trying to keep Fortune Green as an open space, the gipsies became involved in the dispute and their caravans were hauled off the site by protesters.

96. Fortune Green looking south. Following a long legal battle, the Vestry finally bought the Green for a public space, which opened in 1898. Note the children's clothing and the boy pushing his wooden horse along the path.

May your God go with you

The parish church for all of Hampstead was St John's in Church Row. But as the population increased so did the number of churches. The Victorians took religion very seriously and builders saw the provision of a local church as a key attraction of their new developments. Sometimes an estate owner could be induced to donate the site or endow the living. Each new church had a parish allocated to it, with 'mission' churches a feature of less well off neighbourhoods.

Other faiths also looked for sites on which to build their chapels, churches or synagogues. Religion in various forms provided a major source of help to the less privileged members of society in the days before the welfare state.

ST PAUL'S, KILBURN SQUARE

A proprietary chapel was founded near the Cock Inn by local benefactors Francis Nalder of Kilburn House, and Major John Marjoram Close of Kilburn Manor House. On Sunday, 1 March 1829 John Pocock wrote in his diary:

> 'Our new Chapel opened this day. The little village of Kilburn never looked so lively or so proud as on this day, we had an excellent sermon adapted for the occasion by the Rev. Mr Hancock, who is appointed Minister ... We have long wanted a place of worship as the nearest church is distant two miles, the Chapel itself is an elegant, large and commodious structure, the organ a very fine one, the pews well arranged. Altogether it will be a great blessing to the place and is likely to enhance the value of all the property in the neighbourhood.'

About 1835 the chapel was rebuilt as St Paul's Church, Kilburn Square, the only church on the main road between Marble Arch and Edgware. In 1867 the congregation split when Holy Trinity was opened a short distance away in Brondesbury Road. It then went through a lean period until the Rev. George Bonavia-Hunt was appointed vicar in 1887. He was born in Malta but educated

97. St Paul's' Church, Kilburn Square. By 1925 the building was in need of repair but the funds were not forthcoming. It closed in May 1935 and was demolished in 1936.

98. The interior of St Augustine's Church, designed by John Loughborough Pearson.

in London. An accomplished musician, he made St Paul's a centre for church music and he was the founder of Trinity College of Music, London. Many improvements were made to the building and the numbers increased from 20 to 1000. Bonavia-Hunt left Kilburn in 1905 when he moved to Sussex. In 1917 he died of heart failure under anaesthetic during a routine operation.

ST AUGUSTINE'S, KILBURN

St Augustine's Church in Kilburn Park Road, is one of the finest ecclesiastical structures in London, and with the exception of St Paul's and Westminster Abbey, by far the largest. The foundation stone of the nave was laid in May 1876 and the building was consecrated in 1880, though the tower and spire were not completed for another 18 years. It was designed by John Loughborough Pearson at the height of the Catholic Revival. Viscount Rothermere gave the church four paintings, including a Titian, but when one was stolen the rest were sold to prevent further losses.

EMMANUEL CHURCH, LYNCROFT GARDENS

The local population outgrew a mission church in Mill Lane, even after it had been enlarged to seat 400 people in 1884, and a plot of land was bought on the corner of Lyncroft Gardens for a new church. The design was by J.A. Thomas and the builders were Bentley & Sons of Waltham Abbey. The original plan for the church, the first part of which opened in 1898, included an imposing tower and clock, but the funds for these never materialised. A survey in 1903 recorded 765 people attending the church, split between morning and evening services.

The Reverend Davys, the first vicar, was a strong supporter of the Temperance movement and was zealous in promoting what he saw as Christian ideals. George Cross tells how Davys crossed swords with Lieutenant General Fraser, the last occupier of New West End House, who used to hold Sunday parties in the grounds of his house.

> 'This saintly old cleric [Davys] like so many Victorians, my father included, was a strict Sabbatarian, and he looked upon these receptions as orgies which undermined the morals and religion of his flock. One day he called with a triumphant tale to tell. He had written a long letter to General Fraser, pointing out the manner in which he was desecrating the Sabbath and demoralising all the lower orders in the parish, and had ended by saying her Gracious Majesty Queen Victoria would never countenance such entertainments on the Lord's Day.
>
> He had received quite a courteous reply saying the general had no wish to incommode any one in the parish, and that he brought his own staff from town, and that he encouraged all his servants to attend Divine Service at least once on a Sunday, as he did himself whenever possible, but the Vicar was quite in error in stating Her Majesty would not approve or countenance such entertainments, and she had herself given minor functions on a Sunday afternoon.
>
> Then the vicar played his trump card, and chuckled as he recounted it. He had replied to General Fraser that he was evidently misinformed as to the habits of Her Majesty, and he could assure him that the Queen would do no such thing, for it so happened that she had received her early religious instruction from his father, who had been her tutor – and so far as this dear old fellow was concerned, that settled the argument.'

99. The Emmanuel mission church. opened for worship in 1875, on the corner of Aldred Road and Mill Lane.

100. The new Emmanuel Church on the corner of Lyncroft Gardens, which had double the seating of the old mission church. The foundation stone, laid in June 1897, contained a parchment detailing the ceremony and a copy of The Times.

Martin Shaw (1875-1958) was the organist at Emmanuel until 1902, later moving to St Mary's Primrose Hill, and Harold Darke was organist from 1906 to 1911. Both men were distinguished musicians. Shaw's father moved to Hampstead a year after Martin was born, as organist to St John's. Martin was appointed to the first Emmanuel Church in 1894, where he worked hard to develop a good choir. Co-founder of the Purcell Society, he later went on to gain wide recognition as a composer. Harold Darke moved from Emmanuel to St James Paddington and then to St Michael's Cornhill, and in the 1940s was acting organist to King's College Cambridge. President of the Royal College of Organists, a professor at the RCM, Darke also adjudicated at the chief competitive music festivals.

ST MARY'S, ABBEY ROAD

This was one of the few churches in the neighbourhood to be promoted by an estate. In this case it was the developer of the Abbey farm estate, George Duncan, who presented the site, though it was the owner, the Honourable Arthur Upton, who was invited to lay the foundation stone in May 1856. The architects were F. and H. Francis and the church opened the following year at a cost of £4,888.

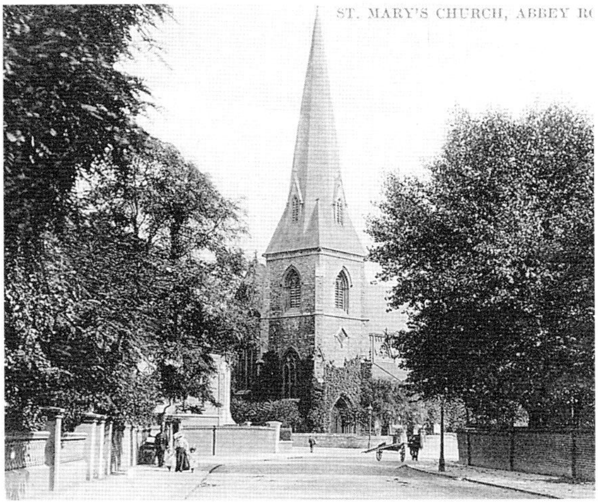

101. St Mary's Church, Abbey Road, consecrated in 1862.

The main structure was completed and consecrated in 1862. The Vicar, the Rev. George Adam, was unable to attend the ceremony due to the death of his eldest daughter Jessy that same day. A stained glass window to her memory was later installed in the Lady Chapel. Rev. Adam was vicar when Thomas Hardy, then living in lodgings on Edgware Road, attended church services at St Mary's. The tower and spire were added in 1872. The vicarage at 50 Priory Road was built by Bayes and Allen in 1876 at a cost of £2,695. The church holds the only known relic of the old Kilburn priory – a small brass plate of one of the prioresses, believed to be Emma de Sancto Omero (*see ill. 4*).

A couple of years after the Rev. Kennion moved into his new vicarage, a diphtheria epidemic hit the neighbourhood. In May 1878 it was reported as 'still hanging about Belsize Road and Kilburn'. That month three young children died at the vicarage – two boys aged seven and two and a girl aged three. At the time no one knew the disease was contagious and it was thought its spread might be due to the escape of sewer gas or defective drains.

ST JAMES, WEST END LANE

St Mary's parish originally stretched as far as the Edgware Road and took in Palmerston Road and the surrounding impoverished streets.

A sad feature of the time was the occasional

102. St James's Church. Designed by A.W. Blomfield, at a cost of £11,750 in 1888, it was built to accommodate a congregation of 1000. Not enough money was raised to build a tower and spire.

unceremonious dumping in the roadway, by the broker's men, regardless of season or weather, of the pitifully scanty household effects of the reckless or unfortunate families who would not or could not pay their rent.

As was often the case in such neighbourhoods, a mission room was established, in this instance at 7 Palmerston Road. Next, a Mission House was built at the corner of Netherwood and Kelson Streets in 1881, at a cost of £4,531.

A site on Sherriff Road facing West End Lane was acquired in 1882 for a new church, St James. A temporary iron church was erected in 1885 but after two years the congregation had expanded to such a degree that it moved into larger rooms in West Hampstead Town Hall next door to the Railway Tavern in Broadhurst Gardens. Finally, the church in Sherriff Road was built in 1887 to the designs of Sir Arthur Blomfield.

103. St Cuthbert's, Fordwych Road (architect W.C. Street), was opened in 1887, providing an attractive vista facing the junction with St Cuthbert's Road. The site was redeveloped in the 1980s to provide a hall, retirement home and a smaller church, opened in 1988.

CHURCHES IN QUEX ROAD

There were at one time three places of worship in Quex Road, though only one, the Sacred Heart Church, now survives. One was the Wesleyan chapel at the corner with Kingsgate Road, designed by J. Tarring. An important landmark, it survived until 1961 when the last service was held in July. By then the congregation had fallen to around 200, and the building could hold more than four times that number. There was no chance to find the £20,000 needed to repair the roof and the minister reported that the pews were up for sale, and he would accept £100 for the organ. The building was subsequently demolished and replaced by a block of flats fronting Quex Road. A much smaller church, with an entrance off Kingsgate Road, opened in 1963.

The land for the Sacred Heart Church in Quex Road was bought in 1866. The Oblates of Mary Immaculate needed a new site for their overcrowded and unhealthy Mission on Tower Hill and they came to Kilburn where half a dozen Catholic families were already established. No. 1 Greville Road became home to a small group of Catholic priests newly arrived in the neighbourhood and for a few years their house served as presbytery and church: 'it was so small that the people had to enter and leave in tiny separate groups'. A temporary chapel was erected in Quex Road in 1868 and the permanent church opened in June 1878. The adjacent 'New Priory' was a home (and a school) for Catholic priests and theology students. The church was well placed to serve the large Irish community of Kilburn which expanded rapidly in post war years. In the 1960s, a series of masses were said each Sunday and it was standing room only.

104. The Wesleyan chapel in Quex Road at the corner of Kingsgate Road, opened in 1869. Methodist services had been previously held at a house in Princess Road, Willesden and then in Belsize Road.

Next door, first a Unitarian Hall and then a Church opened in the 1890s, largely due to the efforts of the Rev. Brooke Herford, who was minister at Rosslyn Hill Chapel. But the congregation had fallen to just 5 in 1965. A year later it was reported Camden was to buy the freehold of the church and hall for £18,200, having prepared plans to demolish the buildings and replace them with a block of flats. The site has since been redeveloped as a group of houses.

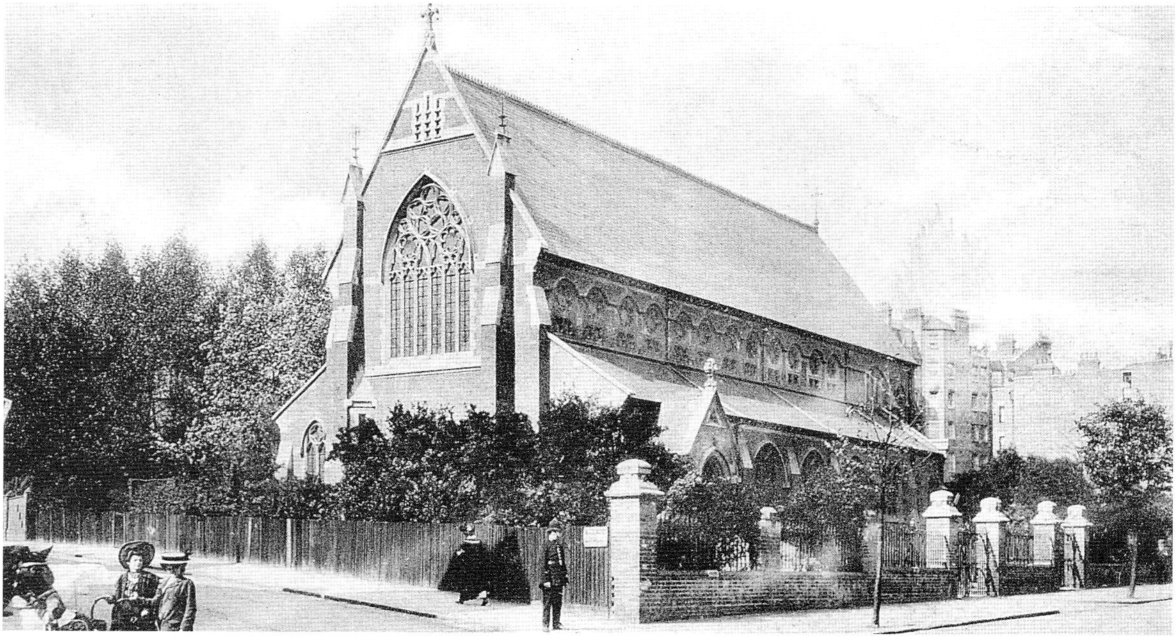

105. Sacred Heart Church was designed by Edward Welby Pugin (who was also responsible for the house called 'The Chimes' next door). Also planned was a 150-ft tower and spire 'to form a conspicuous feature from the wooded heights of Hampstead and Highgate', but this was never built.

THE EBENEZER CHAPEL

The Ebenezer Chapel, off Belsize Road, has a plaque on the door stating that Thomas Creswick preached his last sermon at a bridge near here before his death in 1868. The chapel in his memory was built in 1870 by his sister, who lived nearby in Ebenezer Cottage, Kilburn Vale.

HAMPSTEAD SYNAGOGUE

By the 1880s, there was a large Jewish community in Kilburn and West Hampstead, and in 1890 a suitable site for a synagogue was found:

> After considerable difficulty a site has been secured in West-end-lane, whereon now stands the old ivy covered Lauriston Lodge. The site is central for the West Hampstead, Finchley, Frognal, North Kilburn, Brondesbury, Cricklewood and Willesden districts, and is in a neighbourhood in which the numbers of Jewish residents is constantly and rapidly increasing.

The original plan was for the Synagogue to have 'a handsome and unusual frontage' to West End Lane, with an attractive block of houses and

106. Hampstead Synagogue in Dennington Park Road, opened in 1892.

107. Brondesbury Baptist Chapel on the corner of Iverson Road and Kilburn High Road. The photo looks north and was taken before the Metropolitan Railway bridge was built across the main road.

flats on the corner with Dennington Park Road, incorporating a turret. However, this was abandoned as the Synagogue was turned round to face Dennington Park Road after discussions with the architect, Delissa Joseph, confirmed the opinion that the Ark should be in the east or south-east of the building.

> The plan of the interior is based upon an octagon. The facade is in red brick and red stone and consists of a great central tower, flanked by wings containing the vestibules and by smaller towers enclosing the staircases. The style adopted is Romanesque. It can accommodate 700 worshippers, and fundraising is already well underway.

Ultimately the opportunity to produce an attractive building set in reasonably spacious grounds was lost, as almost every square inch of the site disappeared under bricks and mortar. The rotation of the Synagogue to face Dennington Park Road freed the West End Lane frontage for a row of seven tall shops. The parade was the work of George Neal and called Dennington Promenade: you can still make out the hand painted name above no. 255. There is an interesting stone relief of a faun's face on the facade facing the library, with the date 1892 below.

BRONDESBURY BAPTIST CHAPEL

A Baptist chapel 'with a sugar loaf-spire' was built on the corner of Iverson Road and Kilburn High Road in 1879 with a hall a little way down the road, at nos. 9 and 11. In the early 1980s the chapel was demolished and replaced by sheltered housing, and in 1984 the hall site was also redeveloped to provide a new church, a pastor's flat and five small dwellings.

Leisure Times

WEST END FAIR

An annual fair was held at West End on 26 July and the following two days. It is not known when it began, but probably in the mid to late 1700s. In 1774 an advertisement for it read as follows:

> 'This is to give notice that the Fair will be kept on Wednesday, Thursday, and Friday next, in a pleasant, shady walk, in the middle of the town. On Wednesday a pig will be turned loose, and he that takes it up by the tail and throws it over his head shall have it. To pay twopence entrance, and no less than twelve to enter. On Thursday, a match will be run by two men, a 100 yards, in two sacks, for a large sum. And to encourage the sport the landlord of the inn will give a pair of gloves, to be run for by six men, the winner to have them. And on Friday, a hat, value ten shillings, will be run for by men twelve times round the green; to pay one shilling entrance; no less than four to start. As many as will may enter and the second man to have all the money above four.'

It started in a small way. Germain Lavie of Lauriston Lodge, said that in 1799, when he first came to West End, it had only four or five toy and gingerbread booths and a single show. But it grew, and by 1816 there were 50-60 booths. It was centred around the Green, occasionally spilling over to roadside verges with some stalls set up by villagers in their own front gardens and yards. It became very popular; pubs in Hampstead and Kilburn benefited from passing trade and even set up their own entertainments, while the profit made by the publican at the Cock and Hoop almost paid his annual rent and taxes.

However, the Fair was not popular with most of the wealthier inhabitants, and unsuccessful attempts were first made to stop it in 1812. Then in 1816 Hampstead Vestry was asked to build a new road from West End to Fortune Green, 'for the purpose of having the Fair removed to the latter place.' But agreement could not be reached about who should pay for this.

At the 1819 Fair a riot occurred. On Monday, 26 July a large gang of men, estimated as many as 200, rampaged through the fair, robbing, beating and maltreating anyone they encountered. Bow Street officers and special constables arrived to assist the regular police on Tuesday

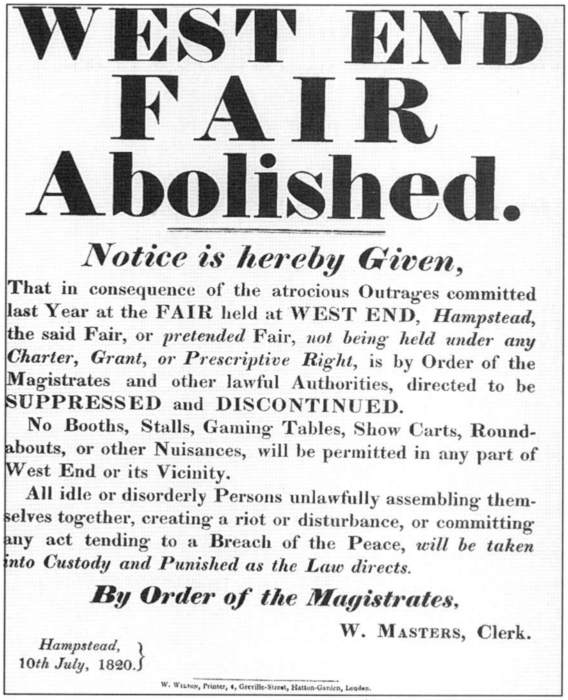

WEST END FAIR Abolished.

Notice is hereby Given,

That in consequence of the atrocious Outrages committed last Year at the FAIR held at WEST END, *Hampstead*, the said Fair, or *pretended* Fair, *not being held under any Charter, Grant, or Prescriptive Right*, is by Order of the Magistrates and other lawful Authorities, directed to be SUPPRESSED and DISCONTINUED.

No Booths, Stalls, Gaming Tables, Show Carts, Roundabouts, or other Nuisances, will be permitted in any part of West End or its Vicinity.

All idle or disorderly Persons unlawfully assembling themselves together, creating a riot or disturbance, or committing any act tending to a Breach of the Peace, *will be taken into Custody and Punished as the Law directs.*

By Order of the Magistrates,

W. MASTERS, Clerk.

Hampstead, 10*th July*, 1820.

W. WILSON, Printer, 4, Greville-Street, Hatton-Garden, London.

108. A handbill of 1820 banning West End Fair.

evening and arrested 30 people. The riot caused an outrage and Germain Lavie, a local magistrate, wrote to the Home Secretary in the strongest terms to get the Fair banned. At least ten people were brought to trial and four were sentenced to death at the Old Bailey for 'highway robbery, accompanied by great violence and outrage'. In the end three were hanged and the other members of the gang were deported to Botany Bay. One of those hanged was not yet 16 and most of them were under 18 years old.

> The leader was hanged in his curled hair, his velveteen coat, his well-fitting cord knee-britches, his striped stockings, his brightly polished high lows, and was exhibited after execution, at a penny a head, by his affectionate parents, in a kitchen in James-street, Oxford-street.

Strenuous efforts were made to suppress the Fair the next year (1820). Policemen and special constables were recruited and stationed on all the approach roads and at local public houses. It is interesting to note that the people signing their names against the Fair were all gentry, while other villagers – who made money from it (including the landlord of the Cock and Hoop), wrote to protest against its cessation. But the gentry had their way and the Fair came to an abrupt end.

THE KILBURN THEATRE ROYAL

The building in Belsize Road which was first opened by Thomas Bate as Kilburn Town Hall in 1876 was rebuilt in 1895 as the Theatre Royal, showing successful West End plays. Some amateur choral and dramatic societies also met there, and 'first class concerts were frequent.' There were two local minstrel troupes, the 'Fireflies' and 'Ohios'. The local Saxby and Farmer Brass Band performed there and public lectures such as that given by Mr Gratton Guinness on a 'New mission to Central Africa' were given. When he talked about Livingstone and Stanley 'a native of the Congoland and an idol were present'. In 1882 the original General Tom Thumb, Major Mite and Commodore Small all appeared at the Town Hall; admission was 6d, one shilling and two shillings.

Charles Landstone, who came to live in the neighbourhood in the late 1890s and went on to make a successful career in theatrical management, claimed that his first visit to this theatre largely determined his future.

> I have been stage-struck ever since I saw my first pantomime at the age of six, in 1897. It was *Dick Whittington* at the Theatre Royal, Kilburn. When the curtain went up for the first time a world opened up to me which has never lost its magic. I had been told to look out for the Cat, and kept on asking in a loud voice where it was, thinking it was of ordinary size and that it might be hidden behind the other people. When it eventually walked on man-size and on all fours I was spellbound, and for the next few months I walked round the dining room on all fours, practising in the hope that someone might call and ask me to play the cat the next year. I saw *Sinbad the Sailor* in the following year and *Little Red Riding Hood* in 1899.

In 1909 the Theatre Royal became a cinema called the Cinematograph Theatre, and later was known as the Kilburn Picture Palace and Theatre of Varieties. After the First World War films were changed twice a week with admission prices ranging from 5d to two shillings and six pence. Sound was introduced in the 1930s, but the Palace closed as a cinema in 1941. By 1953 it had become Shannon's night club and then it was used as a warehouse. During the 1990s it was occupied by Decca Recording Ltd who had moved to Belsize Road in about 1981 from Bate's other property, the old West Hampstead Town Hall in Broadhurst Gardens. Currently the theatre is used as offices.

THE KILBURN EMPIRE

The Empire opened in 1906 at 9-11 The Parade, in the triangle of Kilburn High Road and Kilburn Vale. Designed by W.G.R. Sprague with 1,913 seats, it doubled as a music hall and circus with animal traps and pits. For its first twenty years there were mainly live acts, with some films.

Twice nightly throughout the year, ladies in the Kilburn Empire audience were 'Respectfully Requested to Remove their Hats to Afford a Better View to Persons Seated Behind' of such artists as Natalia and Diana (lady aerial gymnasts) Baby Vi Davis, (wonderful juvenile mime), The Pasquale Boys (World Famous Equilibrists), Joe Archer (the Cheerful Chappie), Ruffells Imperial Bioscope, Rinaldo (the Wandering Violinist), Mooney and Holbein (the Vaudevillians), Flora Cromer (the Lavender Girl), and Jordan and Harvey (Murderers of the Queen's English). Also George Robey, dressed in a shaggy coat as prehistoric man, and the great Marie Lloyd.

The great escapologist Houdini played the Empire in 1909. Ten years later the 'Great Raymond', billed as America's 'Mystery Man' included a séance in his act. An advert was placed in the local newspaper: 'Haunted House wanted. £1000 is offered for a genuine Haunted House or more if the House is worth it.'

In 1927 The Empire began to show films every Sunday, while the variety shows continued during the weekdays. Prices ranged from 6d to two shillings and four pence in the grand circle.

An indication of the poverty in the area in 1927 was shown when 1,100 poor children of the district, most with unemployed fathers, were entertained at the Kilburn Empire with comedy films and a Punch and Judy show. Each child was given a bag containing an apple, an orange, a bar of chocolate, a bun and a rock cake. The following year an advert for the Empire said, 'Every lady should see *The Alluring Stocking* a little film that shows how good stockings are made.' During last war the mix of variety and film at the Empire proved a popular diversion. From 1949 to 1971 it became the Essoldo cinema, which in turn became the Classic Cinema until 1975. The next incarnation was the Broadway Theatre which opened in April 1976 and survived until 1981 showing a mix of Asian language and mainstream films. The World Renewal Spiritual Trust used the building in 1984, and by 1990 you could enjoy a 'paint-ball war game' there. The building was finally demolished in 1994 to make way for the Regents Plaza hotel complex which opened in 1996.

KILBURN ELECTRIC PALACE

This cinema, situated at 10 Kilburn High Road, was opened by Princess Marie Louise of Bourbon on 21 April 1910. She pointed out that previously only the wealthy could see the world, but now thanks to the marvellous invention of cinema 'the most beautiful scenery could be admired for a few pence, while safe from the risks of travelling'. But fierce competition brought an end to this particular Electric Palace, which for a short time from 1914 until it closed in 1916, became the humbler-named 'Cosy Corner Cinema'. In 1917 the corner site became Kilburn Garage which, together with the Kilburn Empire, was demolished in 1994.

THE BIOGRAPH

Converted from trade premises, the Biograph opened as a cinema in 1910. However, it had a short life and closed in 1919, unable to compete with the nearby Grange cinema. During the 1980s the building was used as a recording studio for artists such as Mark Knofler and Eric Clapton. The building still remains behind today's 248 Kilburn High Road.

THE GRANGE CINEMA

After The Grange, the home of the Peters family for many years (*see pp.32-34*), was demolished the cinema of the same name was opened on the site on 30 July 1914. The architect was Edward Stone who designed many other cinemas. With 2,028 seats, a stage, an organ and the Winter Garden café, it was the largest purpose-built cinema of the time. Opening hours were 2.30 to 11 daily and 6 to 10.45 on Sunday. Prices in 1914 were 3d, 6d, and a shilling. At the opening performance the singing of the National Anthem was followed by the film *She Stoops to Conquer* and two short comedies. During the evening there was a recital on the grand organ and an orchestra played in the Winter Garden every evening. In the second week the main attraction was the wonderfully titled, *The World the Flesh and the Devil*. After 60 years the cinema closed. In December 1976 it reopened as the National Club, catering particularly for the area's large Irish community, a venue for showbands and country and western groups. Today, the name of the Grange Cinema still appears in the plaster work and the original stained-glass windows can be seen on the first floor.

MAIDA VALE PICTURE PALACE

The *Kilburn Times* lavished praise on the Maida Vale Picture Palace when it opened in January 1913. Seating 1,500, it was described as London's most luxurious picture theatre with its two imposing towers and coppered domes. The foyer had a marbled floor, the walls were panelled with oak and the colour scheme was royal blue and gold. Performances ran daily from 2.30 to 11pm and were changed twice a week. Admission was from 6d to 2 shillings and a curtained box could be had from seven and sixpence to ten and sixpence. Before the show patrons could

109. The old Grange Cinema, in 1999.

110. *The old Maida Vale Palace, now an Islamic Centre.*

wait in the lounge or the tea room. In 1927 a Grand Wurlitzer organ was installed. The new instrument was so powerful that it could be heard by the residents of Greville Place, three of whom attempted to oppose the renewal of the licence. During the 1920s the cinema gave seasonal children's charity performances, as did the Kilburn Empire. The last films were shown in November 1940 and a restaurant opened the following year. In 1949 it became the Carlton Rooms, a social club and entertainment venue featuring dance bands such as Victor Silvester. When the Mecca Social Club opened in 1961 it was claimed as the first commercial bingo hall in the country; it continued up until 1996. It is now an Islamic Centre.

THE KILBURN STATE

When 'The State' opened on 20 December 1937 with seating for over 4,000 people it was the largest cinema in Europe. Built by its owners, the Hyams brothers, it was claimed that three million bricks were used and that the steel framework for the building weighed 13,000 tons. It was designed by the renowned cinema architect, George Cole. The extravagance of the building attracted 175,000 visitors over the opening days, who marvelled at the foyer, the lush carpets and the mighty Wurlitzer organ. Prices ranged from 6d to three and sixpence. The opening performance starred Gracie Fields, George Formby, Larry Adler and Henry Hall and his Band. It was said to be Queen Mary's favourite cinema and she frequently visited.

The actor Joss Ackland also remembers his visits as a boy:

> Sometimes at the Gaumont State Kilburn as well as all the other goodies before the main feature there would be a bonus of an hour's variety and I can still vividly remember seeing the hilarious Wilson, Keppel and Betty with their Egyptian dance in front of a shaky Pyramids backcloth; Teddy Brown, a gargantuan man playing a delicate xylophone, Harry Tate with his exploding car; the Nicholas brothers all the way from America, who must have been made of India rubber, leaping higher than Nijinsky and further than Jessie Owens, bouncing off and around the auditorium. And then there were ventriloquists, high wire acts, musical saws, conjurors and always lines of beautiful, high-kicking girls.

There were stage shows after the last war, such as Mary Martin in South Pacific. Top rock and roll artists and bands played at the State, including Buddy Holly and the Rolling Stones. When singer and pianist, Jerry Lee Lewis, appeared there in 1958, the press had reported his marriage to his very young cousin, so while half the audience screamed for *Great Balls of Fire*, the other half booed and shouted, 'Go home cradle-snatcher!' The uproar caused him to abandon the show and the whole of his UK tour was cancelled. In 1959 part of the stalls became the Top Rank Ballroom, and as cinema audiences declined the building became a bingo club.

THE CLASSIC CINEMA

In 1939 the Envoy and Television Company opened towards the other end of Kilburn High Road at nos. 403 to 407. By 1954 this was the Envoy Cinema, later called the Classic; it closed in 1980.

THE TRICYCLE

The Theatre opened in 1980 in the old Foresters' Hall. The building was gutted by fire in 1987, and it has since been rebuilt. Designed by Tim Foster, it has a scaffolded auditorium. A recent, and highly successful play was the portrayal of the Stephen Lawrence Enquiry. The Tricycle Cinema was the latest to open in Kilburn in November 1998 at a cost of £3 million. National Lottery funding provided the bulk of the money, but actress Emma Thompson persuaded many celebrities to contribute, among them Dustin Hoffman, Kevin Costner, Arnie Schwarzenegger, Victoria Wood and Joanna Lumley.

111. The unusual entrance passage to the new Tricycle Theatre, 1999.

OTHER DIVERSIONS

A directory for 1929-30 gives the first listing of the 'Acol Social and Bridge Club' at no. 15 Acol Road. The Secretary was a Mr Druiffe who was living in the house before the Club was featured in the directory, so perhaps it was he who brought the players together. According to Ian McLeod in his book *Bridge Is An Easy Game*, published in 1952, the story was as follows:

> Somewhere in Hampstead is an Acol Road. Somewhere in that road used to be, perhaps still is, an Acol Bridge Club. I have never been there. But it was there, nearly twenty years ago that Jack Marx and the late S.J. Simon began to talk over their bridge theories. Bridge in this country was still dominated by one or two West End clubs. Bidding was in its infancy, and the British teams were regularly massacred by American sides. Gradually their ideas developed and began to make headway. I had come down from Cambridge in the summer of 1935 and I met Jack Marx and played in a duplicate pairs with him. So I became the fourth member, (the other was Harrison Grey). Acol was still only a series of ideas unproven in play, unwritten in any Bridge journal. We hammered out our theories in endless sessions night after night into the small hours. The next year we won the main trophy at every Bridge Congress, and all the national team-of-four events for which we entered. Acol had arrived.

Acol is currently on West End Lane, and the actor Omar Sharif, a keen bridge player, is known to have visited the club.

SPORTS

Kilburn was one of the clubs present at the formation of the Football Association in 1863. There were a number of privately owned sports grounds such as the Priory Lawn Tennis Club, behind the present fire station on West End Lane. It numbered amongst its early members Alfred Harmsworth (later Lord Northcliffe) who was then living in Pandora Road. The annual fee was a guinea. There were other courts on the covered Gondar Gardens reservoir and further down West End Lane. In the 1930s, the Mayfair Tennis Club owned by Debenham's stood behind the houses on the south side of Lymington Road while the Imperial Club had courts off Blackburn Road.

112. In 1881 the headquarters of Finchley Harriers was at the Railway Hotel in West End Lane. Every Saturday, the small number of dedicated members would run up the Finchley Road to the fifth mile stone and back to the pub.

113. Hampstead Cricket Club, date unknown. The club moved to Lymington Road in 1877 from St Mary's Fields, behind the church on Abbey Road.

On the Move

THE MAIN ROADS

The road to Edgware has been a main artery out of London since the Romans built it. In the late 19th century, when it became a major shopping area, locally it was renamed Kilburn High Road. From about 1394 right up to the 1860s Willesden Lane was called Mapes Lane, after Walter Map (*c*.1140-1210). Another road led off the Edgware Road towards Kensal Green. This was called Kilburn Lane in 1527 and Flowerhills Lane in 1649. From the top of Shoot Up Hill, Mill Lane led across to West End and on to Hampstead. Blind Lane led off Mill Lane towards Fortune Green.

THE TOLLGATE

Although the Edgware Road benefited from trusts set up by John Lyon (1587) and Edward Harvist (1610), it was used so much that it was 'ruinous and almost impassable' for six months of the year. Use was made unpleasant by heavy wagons, dung heaps at the roadside, encroachments and a shortage of gravel for the road. In 1710, by Act of Parliament, a Turnpike Trust was set up to maintain the road between Kilburn Bridge and Sparrows Hearn, Bushey in Hertfordshire. Trustees were appointed and allowed to erect gates and tollhouses, where vehicles were charged to pass through. When the scheme began in May 1712 the tolls ranged from a shilling for coaches with six horses to a penny for a saddle horse. The rates were increased over time so that the six-horse coach was charged one shilling and six pence in 1789 and two shillings by 1819, while the single horse rate changed to twopence.

Long distance coaches regularly travelled through Kilburn, encouraging the establishment of large numbers of inns and taverns. In 1768 a daily stage coach ran from London along the Edgware Road and by 1828 you could catch four local coaches a day from Kilburn to Oxford Street and the Bank. John Pocock had to walk home carrying a heavy bible one cold evening in February 'as the Kilburn stage passed me quite full'. In practice, however, high fares and infrequent services meant they were of limited use. John thought nothing of walking long distances to Charing Cross, Brixton or Southwark, and even as far as Hastings on one occasion, sometimes using field paths as short cuts.

114. The main tollgate on Kilburn High Road, shown here, was situated just north of Kilburn Bridge, and there were sidebars on the roads that led off to Kensal Grove and to West End. In 1864 the Kilburn tollgate was moved to the end of Willesden Lane and then again to Shoot Up Hill, where it remained until the road ceased to be turnpiked in 1872.

'Left Smoke and London with Josiah this morning for a long walk. We took the Whitechapel road and went first to Bow with its Church. I was very much pleased because of its antiquity. We then took a circuitous route to Hadley where we had a pleasant view with the telescope. We enjoyed our walk very much, it must have been easily thirty miles.

On the rare occasion he took the coach, he was usually accompanying one of his parents: 'rode from Maida Hill to Fleet Market in one of St Albans long-stages with my mother – we were terribly jolted over the stones'. He witnessed one of the earliest experiments in powered locomotion when one of Sir Goldsworth Gurney's steam carriages travelled up the Edgware Road 'in style', as John put it, on 19 January 1828.

The Finchley Road from St John's Wood to Finchley was completed in 1829, but in an age of primitive transport it does not seem to have immediately affected the development of West End. For the time being, living in outlying places such as the new Kilburn Priory houses or the even remoter West End was impractical for anyone who wanted to travel regularly to London for business, even if they were wealthy enough to run their own coach. Poor road surfaces and the length of the journey ruled it out.

The first omnibus service in London was begun along the New Road (today's Marylebone, Euston and Pentonville Roads) in 1829, but it took several years before services extended up the Edgware Road and far longer to reach West End Green. In 1838 one bus went to Kilburn, but by 1856 there were upwards of 22 running to and from the Kilburn Gate. In 1880 there were also three routes leaving from either the Lord Palmerston pub or The Cock. Buses ran at six to fifteen minute intervals, serving Charing Cross, London Bridge and Victoria. Services were soon extended to Cricklewood but residents in West End had to wait until the 1890s.

Horse buses were limited by the ability of two animals to pull a car much further than six miles in a single journey. And there had to be stables at both ends of a route. Companies competed for custom along all the major roads and in the 1890s it was estimated that the largest of them, the London General Omnibus Company, had 10,000 horses working a thousand buses, carrying one hundred and ten million passengers a year. A yard was established behind the Lord Palmerston and another off Kingsgate Road, and when the buses finally reached West End Green, an open space round the corner in Mill Lane was purchased and equipped. It was the by-product of the trade that caused most problems – the many tons of manure that needed daily removal. In 1873, residents in Palmerston Road complained of the 'foul and offensive state' of the bus yard. The following year the Medical Officer of Health reported that:

Forty or fifty horses were kept in old stables badly paved through years of dung saturated soil; that the dung bins and other surroundings were very offensive; that a notice should be served on the bus proprietors to make the stables pure.

There were no official stops for many years other than the termini. A passenger simply held up his or her hand and the bus stopped. A local resident, Charles Landstone, who lived in Plympton Road, described the High Road in the late 1890s.

Here the horse-buses plied busily. There was rivalry between the bus companies, the two main contenders being the London General Omnibus Company (in red) and the London Red Car Company (in chocolate.). Chariot races worthy of a Roman stadium used to take place down the High Road. I can remember reading in the *Kilburn Times* a solemn warning against the danger to life and limb caused by this foolish competition.

Buses were joined on London's roads by horse trams from 1869. The permission of the local authority was needed before tram companies could lay rails on a public road and Hampstead consistently refused to sanction any lines inside its boundaries. From the outset, the tram was viewed as a working class form of transport. Their fares were such that a poorer class of traveller could afford to use them; in any case most companies were required by law to run a 'workmen's service' between certain hours and charge a statutory fare. This explains why just one line running through the working class streets of Kentish Town was reluctantly permitted to terminate at South End Green. In 1878 the Vestry concluded that the tramway schemes 'proposed to be introduced to this parish will destroy the character of the several roads proposed to be traversed and that such schemes are opposed to the wishes of the inhabitants generally'.

115. Midland Station, West End Lane.

RAILWAYS

The railways undoubtedly had the greatest effect on the neighbourhood. The fields of Kilburn and West Hampstead were criss-crossed by tracks and, had their promoters prevailed, there would have been even more. Standing in Iverson Road today and looking across the deep cutting to the rear of the houses in Sumatra Road, it is hard to believe this was once level ground with a slight slope towards Kilburn High Road. Millions of tons of earth were excavated and removed here, along with several other sites in the neighbourhood.

Local services took a while to develop, as the pioneer lines arrived well in advance of any suburban market. Their role was long distance traffic, in and out of a central London terminus. The first was the London & Birmingham line, later renamed the London & North Western Railway (LNWR).

A station was opened in Belsize Road in 1852 with a second exit to the High Road in 1879. This was followed in 1860 by the Hampstead Junction Railway (HJR) later known as the North London line, with a station on Kilburn High Road. Lack of local traffic meant the company did not bother opening a station on West End Lane until 1888. During the sixties the Midland Line swept in a wide arc across and under the HJR line from Finchley Road north to Cricklewood. A purpose built station already existed in Iverson Road, in one of the three large villas erected on spec a few years earlier. Opened in 1868 it was later replaced by a station facing West End Lane.

In 1879 the Metropolitan & St John's Wood Railway extended north and westwards to Willesden Green from its terminus at Swiss Cottage, opening stations at Finchley Road, West Hampstead and Kilburn. In the 1930s a new stretch of tube line – the Bakerloo – was built from Baker Street to Finchley Road, where it took over two of the Metropolitan's old tracks. New platforms at West Hampstead opened in 1938.

During the 1860s, the progress of works involved in building the Midland's extension to St Pancras was closely monitored by Hampstead Vestry. It didn't debate engineering matters but concentrated instead on the problems caused by the large numbers of navvies employed to build the line by Joseph Firbank the contractor. Attention focused on their living conditions. While nothing out of the ordinary for itinerant labourers, they were often insanitary and sometimes lethal. Whole families accompanied the navvies,

116. West Hampstead was the scene of a major railway accident, when on a foggy morning in October 1907 a northbound Metropolitan train ploughed into the back of one at the station. Three men were killed. A signalman was later charged with manslaughter but acquitted.

either camping out in the open fields bordering the tracks or using whatever rented accommodation they could.

Firbank was no philanthropist. He built a number of two-room huts as temporary accommodation for his men in the fields and charged them six shillings a week rent. In return he supplied free coal and furniture. There were 15 huts off Finchley Road on the edge of two open sewers, lacking either proper drainage or a water supply, their inhabitants relying instead on open privies. A further 13 cottages stood near Mill Lane. In November 1865, in an apparent attempt to reduce overcrowding, notice was given to the hut dwellers, forbidding them to take in more than six lodgers, (previously eight had been the limit and in some cases more).

But a visit to the huts in January 1866 revealed that overcrowding was still rife. It was reported in some cases 'relays of men appeared to occupy the beds by day that had been occupied by night' (known as the 'hot bed' system). The hot summer months brought fresh problems for the Medical Officer of Health when smallpox broke out in the huts near Mill Lane: 'the crowded and ill constructed the huts used by the navvies and brickmakers still caused him much alarm, and demanded constant vigilance'.

The unfortunate navvies had a rotten life. The temporary nature of their work meant they were constantly on the move around the country, surviving as best they could. The work was often dangerous and the inhabitants disliked them. Their only local champion was the Reverend Sharpe, subsequently vicar of Holy Trinity Church, Finchley Road. He helped the men and even held the odd service in the tunnel under Haverstock Hill.

In 1881 an intriguing story appeared in the *Kilburn Times* when they reported that 'Diogenes is dead'. They pointed out that it was not the ancient Greek philosopher, but a pretty pink-eyed white haired rat who lived beneath the platform of Kilburn Station and who ate the scraps which passengers threw to him. The station master's cat, Nemesis, seized him and killed him, but the murder was quickly avenged as Nemesis was killed by a train.

In March 1906 two carriages of the Metropolitan Railway caught fire at West Hampstead Station. The front and rear coaches had an apparatus that connected to the live rail and transformed the electricity for the motor. The train was full of passengers but there were no injuries. Although they caught fire, the carriages were fireproofed and had concreted floors.

Commuter numbers grew unevenly but substantially during the inter-war years, but persistently low ticket sales led the Midland to shut its station on Finchley Road in 1927. In general, the lines sustained surprisingly little damage from enemy bombing during the last war. Since then, the North London line has been under frequent threat of closure while in 1962 the Midland station was described as a 'gloomy ruin'.

Sales of land originally used for sidings and shunting but now surplus to requirements have occurred, notably for public housing (West End Sidings estate) and shops (the recently opened O_2 centre on Finchley Road). Services on both the Silverlink and Thameslink have increased and diversified with new links established in recent years, but commuter complaints of overcrowding and unreliability are frequent, especially on Thameslink. In 1978 a plan was put forward to create a new interchange at West Hampstead, one option being to link all three stations on the west side of the Lane. In 1998 plans were again proposed by Railtrack for a new 'super station' at West Hampstead, but the exact location and form the development will take, if indeed it goes ahead, have yet to be decided.

THE BICYCLE AND THE CAR

The 1890s witnessed the start of a revolution in personal transport: the bicycle, followed by the car. George Cross remembered what it was like.

> By 1895 if you had not a bicycle you were beyond the pale. Everybody was buying them and learning to ride, and the learning to ride was a serious business. There were actually professional teachers. In every quiet side street in the evening you would see fat old ladies being supported and shoved along by their perspiring mates, fathers by their sons, daughters by their sweethearts.

In 1898 the Vestry issued a prophetic report concerning the second new invention.

> The utility of the motor car is not yet assured. The time, therefore, for its common use in business cannot be foreseen, but with so much attention devoted to it, with a view to perfecting the machine, that time may be nearer than is generally thought.

The motor car arrived at the beginning of the century. The excitement of seeing the new invention is captured by a young boy:

> One morning in the High Road towards the turn of the century, when I was accompanying my mother on a shopping expedition, I saw in the distance a cloud of billowing black smoke. Everyone was gaping and staring, buses reared to the side of the road, and drivers of stationary carts rushed to hold the heads of their panic-stricken horses. Emitting puffs and pants, the smoke cloud drew nearer along the road. "Look Charley", cried my mother excitedly, "it's a motor-car!" I had never heard the word before but I watched with passionate interest as out of the smoke there emerged the shape of a curious vehicle which miraculously, without the aid of any horse, was moving along the road at the rate of at least ten miles an hour.

Two motor bus routes were introduced to Kilburn in September 1910 when it was reported that this 'busy thriving district' had been without direct motor buses to the City, Waterloo or the West End since the withdrawal of horse bus services a year ago. Among the several routes on offer were the number 16 from Cricklewood to Victoria and the 8 from Willesden to the Bank and Seven Kings, costing 8d to travel 17 miles. 1910 also saw one of the first motor fatalities in the district at the bend of Lymington Road, where a car knocked down and fatally injured an old lady. To his horror the driver found he had hit his own grandmother! By 1911 and 1912 complaints were being made of 'heavy motor and motor bus traffic' on Abbey Road and West End Lane, resulting in general property depreciation as well as damage to both road surfaces and foundations due to excessive vibration. The speed of the traffic was also criticised. It soon became necessary to install traffic lights at busy junctions.

Almost no new roads have been built since the main street network was established by the Victorians and early Edwardians. And until recently most changes were concerned with improving traffic flow, such as the widening of Finchley Road to a six lane highway. While the car is still seen as an important adjunct to modern living, in recent years attempts have been made to redress the balance. Parking restrictions and 'traffic calming' schemes have been introduced to help reclaim local streets for residents and pedestrians. But when they were first suggested back in the 1970s not everyone could see the point. A traffic scheme to stop cars from 'rat-running' between Kilburn High Road and West End Lane met with scant interest or support from the locals in 1975.

If the planners had had their way thirty years ago, the face of modern Kilburn and West Hampstead would be very different. The planned

117. There was a cycle shop on West End Lane with the wonderful name of Delevante and Co. Mr Delevante had invented the 'Princess Cycle – well known to metropolitan riders and especially on the north road'. He also sold tandems and tricycles, hired machines and offered tuition.

Ringway One, the Motorway Box, involved a six-lane highway from the end of the M1 near Brent Cross, south along the Camden side of Edgware Road where it followed the line of the old Midland Railway to a huge ten-lane interchange at the junction of Fordwych and Maygrove Roads. From here one road went east to a link with the A40, the other west to cross Finchley Road and over to Belsize Park and Chalk Farm. The road was to be variously elevated, in a cutting or enclosed. The public enquiry began in 1971 and the following year the local paper warned of the dangers of low public awareness: 'some pro-motorway enthusiasts misguidedly equate public apathy as a sign of approval'. Over a thousand properties lay in its path while upwards of 17,500 residents would be either displaced or affected by noise and pollution. Protesters argued that 'the western side of Finchley Road would present a pretty bleak and dreary picture of the exposed underside of the descending motorway' while supporters said such a road would siphon off heavy traffic from local and residential streets. The scheme was abandoned due to escalating protests and spiralling costs, and this victory was seen as a move away from a car dominated society, to one where public transport played a primary role. Thirty years on we have yet to realise this dream.

Places of Learning

An 1835 survey of Hampstead noted that the Kilburn Infant School had been opened that year to take 47 children. There was also one day and one Sunday School begun in 1829, for 45 boys and 40 girls, while a class of 16 girls received free education on Sunday from a lady at her own Kilburn home.

The Education Act of 1870 ensured that elementary schools would be built where provision from other sources – for example, parochial schools – was insufficient. These were known as Board Schools and until 1891 they charged fees. In 1918 the school leaving age was raised from 12 to 14, but even then not everyone could afford to go on to secondary education, for which fees were only abolished in 1944. Many local children took up full time employment instead.

The earliest education provided for the village children at West End was probably a Dame School run by Hannah Bowstead from her home in Alpha Cottage in West End Lane (now buried under Inglewood Mansions). It catered for some twenty or so children. The opening of Emmanuel School would have reduced but perhaps not destroyed her business entirely.

HOLY TRINITY SCHOOL, KILBURN

Holy Trinity School was erected on the site of the old parish pond and pound where Victoria Road is today. Willesden Vestry minutes for 25 May 1843 record that the site was given to the church for the erection of the school by public subscription. It was erected in memory of Rev. W. Hancock, the first vicar of St Paul's chapel, and in the 1850s it had 248 pupils. In 1867 the school came under Holy Trinity Church in Brondesbury Road. It closed in 1926 and the present building on the site, Trinity House, is a reminder of the old name.

118. Holy Trinity School stood next to the Victoria Rifle Ground on Kilburn High Road.

119. The Emmanuel school yard.

EMMANUEL SCHOOL

Emmanuel School was opened in 1846 on the same site it occupies today and is the oldest surviving building in West Hampstead. The architect was Charles Miles, the son of the owners of nearby West End House. His parents were the prime movers behind the scheme to provide a school for the villagers. The original one classroom for 143 children and the cottage for the teacher were enlarged in 1874 and a new cottage built two years later; there were further extensions in 1890.

An ex-pupil from 1916 remembers:

> 'The school rooms were heated in winter by coal fires – large square, iron free-standing affairs, with tall chimneys through the ceilings. Lighting was by gas. Every morning began with a devotional session, followed by a Scripture lesson before we went on to other subjects. For the top classes, cookery lessons were held at Kingsgate Road School which was quite a walk. For laundry classes we went to Broomsleigh Street School. Housewifery was taught at Berridge House. I have been told that some years before I was there part of Friday afternoons was spent learning to mend – darning, patching etc. We walked in a crocodile to the hall at the corner of Dornfell Street for drill and dancing classes. For swimming we went to the baths in Finchley Road. The senior classes walked to the Heath to play netball.'

The school always suffered from lack of space. The small plot it occupied was very cramped, a fact already recognised back in 1896, when a favourable report on the school and its pupils' abilities concluded, 'the accommodation is at present insufficient for the average attendance.' After the last war, it was decided to use the old bus depot across West End Lane, behind Cavendish Mansions, as the site for a new Emmanuel School. Work was expected to begin in the early 1970s, but falling school rolls led to the scheme being shelved indefinitely.

ST MARY'S

The first St Mary's school was established on a site off Kilburn Priory by the railway line. In 1869 General Upton (the owner of the Abbey Farm estate) paid £510 for the freehold of a site in West End Lane, just off Kilburn High Road, with the proviso that a new school be built there to replace the 'incommodious one' already existing – this served St Paul's Chapel across the way in Kilburn Square. Built by Manley and Rogers at a cost of £1,648, the school opened in 1870.

Over the years the buildings were extended and improved but the site was very restricted. It was not until November 1991 that a new school was opened at the corner of Quex Road and West End Lane. It was designed by Professor Hans Haenlein and is one of the most modern in the country. The hall is in a central covered courtyard with a slide-back roof, the classrooms opening off the hall on three sides. Ex-pupils include the actor Peter Egan and Fred Housego, the taxi-driver who won the BBC Mastermind competition.

BECKFORD SCHOOL

Emmanuel School clearly could not cope with the large numbers of children from the many new streets in West Hampstead. So the site for Beckford School (originally called Broomsleigh Street School until 1931 when it was renamed after the owner of Old West End House) was made the subject of a compulsory purchase order in 1884. The land cost £2,850 and the buildings another £10,000. When it opened in 1886, the school could accommodate 793 pupils, including 25 transferred from Emmanuel. It was enlarged to take nearly double that number by 1894.

The fees were set at 3d per child or 2d for each subsequent child from the same family, and infants paid 2d. Practical skills such as shorthand, woodwork, knitting and laundry work were taught as well as the usual academic subjects. The girls were also taught how to cook at Netherwood School and later at Berridge House on Fortune Green Road. Past pupils include the actors Joss Ackland and Emma Thompson.

KINGSGATE SCHOOL, KINGSGATE ROAD

This Board School opened in 1903 on land once part of the neighbouring Grange Estate. The corner plot with Kingsgate Road was made the subject of a compulsory purchase order, but rented back to Mrs Peters, the owner of The Grange, until required. But in 1902 the School Board was forced to take her to court to obtain possession; the judge accurately summed up the situation when he concluded that, 'the lady still thought the land was hers, though she had sold it and got a fair price for it'.

120. A class at Kingsgate School on Empire Day, 1928.

HABERDASHERS' ASKE'S

In 1898 Haberdashers' Aske's School was searching for a site for a boys' school in West Hampstead. It bought land in Westbere Road about 1901, and unlike the often unpopular board school, its arrival was welcomed. The first building was opened in 1902 and others followed. The school was intended to take about 300 pupils.

> The cost of the site and buildings for the school not to exceed £32,000. Further the age of the scholars shall be between 8 and 17 years of age, and a preparatory branch may be added for boys between 5 and 8 years of age; that the tuition shall be at the rate if not less than £4 and not more than £8 a year for each scholar, and that several important scholarships and exhibitions shall be granted to scholars in the school.

Haberdashers' moved to Hertfordshire in 1961 and the building now houses Hampstead Comprehensive.

KILBURN GRAMMAR SCHOOL

Dr. George Bonavia Hunt (1847-1917), the vicar at St Paul's, founded a boys' choir school in 1897 at 1 Willesden Lane, which moved to Cavendish Road a year later. In 1900 it became Kilburn Grammar School for Boys and moved into purpose-built buildings at the top of Salusbury Road, opposite Brondesbury and Kilburn High School for Girls. Dr Hunt, who taught musical history at the University of London, was there until 1904. The roll in 1900 was 120 and the school was enlarged in 1927 under the Middlesex County Council. It suffered some war damage and was re-built in 1957. In 1967 the boys' and girls' schools were amalgamated to form Brondesbury and Kilburn High School, which closed in 1989.

Kilburn Grammar School provided a way into university and successful careers. Richard Baker, the BBC newsreader and broadcaster was at the school. In the 1950s he agreed to rent a flat at 32 Dennington Park Road but gave up, as it seemed impossible to get his piano up the stairs to the first floor. Other ex-pupils include Kenneth Howard, an artist who painted for the British Army from the 1970s; the linguist, Professor Simeon Potter, who also wrote a history of Willesden, and many other people listed in *Who's Who*, now holding positions such as an Air Chief Marshal, professors, high-level civil servants, judges and company directors.

Ex-pupils from the girls' high school also achieved success. 'Twiggy' or Lesley Hornby, became an internationally famous model in the 1960s. Margery Hurst, founded the Brook Street Bureau, a well-known employment agency. She was the managing director and when it was sold for nearly £20 million in 1985 she became chairman until ill-health forced her to resign in 1988. Another entrepreneurial woman was Doreen Miller, chairman and managing director of the cosmetics company Universal Beauty Club. She was created Baroness Miller of Hendon in 1993.

PRIVATE SCHOOLS

The neighbourhood was also once home to a large number of private schools.

Charles Landstone recalls his childhood days in Kilburn at the turn of the century and attempts to explain why there were so many educational establishments.

> After we had moved there came the question of schooling. It was a snobbish period. State schools – or board schools as they were then known – were only patronised by the artisan class, and everybody else, even the lowest grade of white-collar worker, paid for their children's education.

From 1899 onwards he attended Brondesbury College which had moved from Quex Road to Willesden Lane.

> Mr Potbury, the owner and headmaster, had good scholastic qualifications. It was a huge Victorian house with a basement and at least four floors above, and I think there must have been about sixty boys. The tuition was good – there were about four assistant masters – and the boys were, like myself, good solid lower middle-class. I left in 1902 and went to a public secondary day school, the Haberdashers' [in Westbere Road]. My school fellows were mostly the sons of shopkeepers.

St Winifred's was a well-known girls' private school at 139 West End Lane, between Dynham and Hemstal Roads. It was begun by Miss Smorthwaite in 1877. When she died in 1905 the new principal was Miss Chaplin who had been a pupil at the school. That year they opened a kindergarten class for boys as well as girls.

121. York House School, 1 Crediton Hill. 'Their blazers, caps, ties and sock tops were green and mauve. Two women taught the younger boys and administered discipline with the aid of an old gym slipper.

THE ANGLO FRENCH COLLEGE

In 1867 James Haysman leased Temple Park, the Burgess family mansion, which was more than large enough to accommodate both his college and his family. He called his new enterprise the Anglo French College, reflecting his belief that education should place as much emphasis on teaching modern language skills as other standard subjects. Provision was made for his pupils to study abroad, but Haysman had to overcome prejudice: 'The British parent seemed to have an inherent dread of sending their boys abroad, seeming to think that Boulogne or Bonn are as remote as Timbuktu'. The school housed an average of eighty boarders, all boys aged between 8 and 17, and day pupils were also welcomed.

Haysman prospered and opened his second commercial undertaking, the International College at the corner of Finchley and Lymington Roads in 1886. He continued to run both academic establishments in tandem until 1895 when his Temple Park lease finally expired.

FIELD LANE INDUSTRIAL SCHOOL, HILLFIELD ROAD

West Hampstead was also home to a very different establishment, some ten minutes down the hill from Haysman's college. The Industrial School in Hillfield Road opened in 1878 as a branch of the Field Lane Refuge in Holborn. Pupils were usually sent to the school by magistrates in an attempt to get them away from an undesirable family background so they could earn a trade. These were boys who:

122. The Field Lane Industrial School was obliged to move out of central London in 1878. The girl pupils moved to Church Row, Hampstead, and the boys to Hillfield Road (depicted here). The school was closed in 1931.

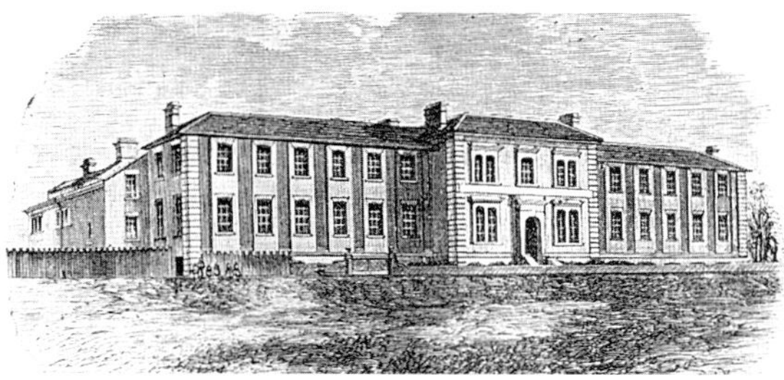

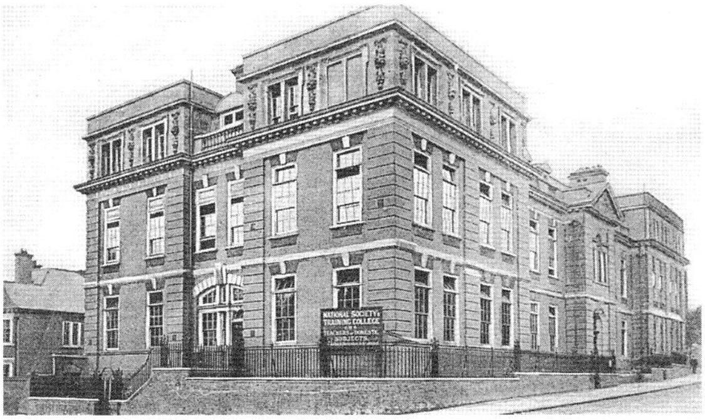

123. Berridge House, on the corner of Hillfield and Fortune Green Roads.

> At ages ranging from but little above infancy to the more mature period marked by sixteen years' experience of life, have established themselves as incorrigible truants from school, petty thieves, or bold adventurers of the Jack Sheppard type, and have, as a result of these characteristics, made their appearance as prisoners.

The Hillfield Road school could take up to a hundred boys and was usually full. It aimed to completely rehabilitate the boys by combining academic and practical skills, the latter including gardening, baking, tailoring and shoemaking to craftsman level. The school band gave annual concerts on Fortune Green, sometimes to raise funds for a seaside holiday for the boys.

However laudable the aims of the Industrial School movement, it was not always regarded well by outsiders: the locals usually referred to the establishment as 'the bad boys' school'.

BERRIDGE HOUSE

In 1909 a second educational establishment was opened on land between the Field Lane School buildings and Fortune Green Road, originally used by the boys of the Industrial School as a playground. This was Berridge House, a training college for teachers of Domestic Science.

In the 1950s it was common to see the students carrying covered but steaming dishes of hot food out of the main entrance in Fortune Green Road – presumably the end product of a day's labour being taken back to their digs round the corner for supper! When the Field Lane School closed in 1932, Berridge House bought its building to use as an accommodation block. It survived until recently, still used as student housing, latterly for Westfield College. Since then the grounds have been replaced by Berridge Mews, and in1966 Berridge House was demolished to build the new West Hampstead Police Station.

124. The St John's Foundation School, Mortimer Road. The illustration dates from 1857, a year after the school's foundation. It offered an education to poor Church of England clergymen's sons.

125. The Queen's Arms, Kilburn High Road, once a tavern, was transformed into a hotel. It had pleasure gardens sloping down to the Kilbourne stream which flowed under the bridge. One resident remembers that in the 1830s 'it was largely patronised by young dancing people'.

Drinking Places

Kilburn, which catered for a great deal of passing traffic on the Edgware Road, had drinking places from Tudor times. Some were *bona fide* inns, others just beerhouses, usually in a small cottage. Beer was often made on the premises by women and as often as not sold by them while their husbands had jobs outside the home. Sometimes the pub was also the local store, selling basic groceries and even drinking water.

On the Hampstead side of Kilburn High Road, the Red Lion, the Bell, the Black Lion, the Coopers Arms, the Sir Colin Campbell and Lord Palmerston public houses have endured, while beerhouses including the intriguingly named Help the Lame Dog Over the Stile came and went. On the Willesden side were the Queen's Arms, The Volunteer, The Cock, the Earl Derby, and the Victoria Tavern.

The public houses also served as hotels or meeting places, with rooms for hire for functions. They also provided space for auction sales of land following demolition of local mansions. Also, coroners held inquests in them and at times they were even used as makeshift mortuaries.

In a Middlesex Sessions Roll of 1552 there was only one (unnamed) alehouse in Kilburn, and in 1613 still only one licensed tippler, George Flower. He was also sworn in as a constable. By 1872 there were eight public houses in Kilburn High Road, and another thirteen in the surrounding streets. In addition, there were two beer retailers in the High Road and two more in the side roads.

THE COCK

The Cock claims to have received its licence in 1486, although licensing by magistrates did not begin until 1495. In the 1830s there were Sunday afternoon meetings there to discuss the science of boxing as the licensee's brother was the pugilist, Tom Cribb. Behind the Cock were cottages and gardens which survived until 1925. The original Cock was burnt down and rebuilt about 1794.

VICTORIA TAVERN

Situated on the corner of Willesden Lane and the High Road, The Victoria Tavern was previously called the 'Alec Keene' after a well know prize fighter. Currently it is called Biddy Mulligan's.

126. (Above) The Old Bell, Kilburn High Road, probably dates from the 17th century. At one time the landlord also ran the Kilburn Wells and there were popular tea gardens at the back of the pub. In 1863 the pub was pulled down and the present building erected.

127. (Below)The Canterbury Arms, 111 Canterbury Road, faced the large Saxby & Farmer signal works. The Royal Mail sorting office in Coventry Close occupies part of the site today.

128. Jumbo Eccleston, the landlord of the Canterbury Arms, claimed to be the second heaviest man in the world in the 1890s. He had a special pony and trap to travel in.

129. *An undated watercolour of The Cock on Kilburn High Road.*

RAILWAY HOTEL, WEST END LANE

The Railway Hotel was opened by Richard Pincham in 1881. The following year he was awakened in the night by the barking of his dog. Armed with his six-chamber revolver he heard a low whistle and saw burglars scrambling away near his stables. He fired once but the men made good their escape.

In the 1960s it was the venue of Klook's Kleek, a jazz and blues club where the top American and British bands played. Recordings were conveniently made by running a cable through to the Decca studios next door. The pub has recently been modernised and named the Rat and Parrot to attract a younger clientele.

IN WEST END

The village of West End had a beerhouse, the Old Black Horse, and surprisingly for such a small village, two pubs, the Old Black Lion and the Cock and Hoop. This may have been due to trade connected with the annual Fair. Up the road the Prince of Wales by Fortune Green began life as a beerhouse.

In 1878 a local newspaper reported the following incident relating to the Cock and Hoop:

> A white bull terrier with tan spots, apparently rabid, entered the bedroom of the landlord of the Cock and Hoop pub at West End Green where it tore some bedclothes. It was chased out and went up the road to Mr Cotching's farm where it bit his dog. It then entered Mr Winyard's house near The Old Black Lion pub where it killed his cat before running away south down West End Lane and escaping, but not before it bit William Cleaver, the engine boy at the Midland Station.

The villagers kept their cricket bats and wickets in the pub, and with permission from their employers to leave work early, they went to Fortune Green to play a game in teams of 'marrieds' versus 'singles'.

The proximity of the pub and the temptation presented by the 'demon drink' were a source of great concern to the congregation of nearby Emmanuel Church. In 1896 the authorities closed the pub when it was discovered that the named licensee, Mr Robinson, had been dead for four years! Whether a victory for temperance or not, the Cock and Hoop never reopened. Alexandra Mansions, built in 1902, stand on the site today.

130. Possibly dating from as early as the mid fifteenth century, the Red Lion, Kilburn High Road, was rebuilt in 1890. It has recently been redecorated and a capstone showing the date 1444 can be seen at the top of the building. The painting is by local resident, John Rathbone.

131. A watercolour of the Black Lion, Kilburn High Road, by Appleton.

132. *The present building of the Cock Tavern. It dates from 1900.*

CRICKET.

A MATCH

WILL BE PLAYED ON THE

BLACK LION GROUND,

KILBURN,

On Monday, June 12th, 1854,

Between Eleven Players of the Young Eagle Cricket Club, Hackney, & Eleven Players of the Black Lion Perseverance Club, Kilburn.

Wickets to be Pitched at Eleven o'clock.

REFRESHMENTS ON THE GROUND

OF THE BEST QUALITY.

134. *Poster advertsing a cricket match at the Black Lion, Kilburn in 1854.*

133. *Originally opened as the Palmerston Hotel, it later became the Lord Palmerston and a landmark as a terminus for several horse bus services. The pub was closed in May 1977 and reopened as the Roman Way, presumably referring to Watling Street. The current manifestation is Nando's restaurant.*

135. Watercolour of the Cock and Hoop, West End Lane, north of the Green, by T.T. Wilson, 1869. In existence by 1723, it was the larger of the two pubs at West End. There was a quoits and skittle ground in the field behind, and the landlord put on special entertainments during the West End Fair.

136. Watercolour of the Old Black Lion, West End Lane, by T.T. Wilson, 1896. It shows the bluff wall of Inglewood Mansions on the left. In 1914 a group calling themselves the 'Excelsior Musical Society' gave concerts here. For a short time in 1998 it was given the name of 'Rat and Carrot, but this was so unpopular that the old name has been restored.

Famous Names

SOME EARLY RESIDENTS
The rural charms of Kilburn and West Hampstead attracted a number of wealthy residents during the nineteenth century. Many were self-made men who may have felt comfortable in this more relaxed neighbourhood, where 'earned' money was not looked down upon. Neither district attracted the numbers of artists, poets and writers who made Hampstead and Highgate their homes, but many of them were regular visitors. Constable painted the meadows in West End and Kilburn Mill, while Leigh Hunt rented a small cottage near the Green for a few months. In the summer of 1819 John Keats and his friend, the painter Benjamin Haydon, were walking through Kilburn Meadows. It was here that Keats recited his newly composed *Ode to a Nightingale*, 'with a tremulous under tone', to Haydon.

Samuel Chappell, 20 Greville Place, the music shop owner.

In January 1811, the original partners in the firm of Chappell and Co – Samuel Chappell and the musicians, John Baptist Cramer and Francis Tatton Latour – opened their shop at 124 Bond Street. Soon the firm made its influence felt in music publishing. In 1822, Beethoven, writing from Vienna to his friend Ferdinand Ries in London, commented 'Potter says that Chappell in Bond Street is now one of the best publishers.' Samuel Chappell moved the business to 60 New Bond Street. The firm later became known for arranging public readings by Charles Dickens.

Cantelo Bestland an artist, lived at '2 The Green' (1795-*c*.1828), a terrace of three houses opposite West End Green on the site of the present Pizza Express. He was a talented engraver, print publisher and miniaturist who exhibited at the Royal Academy and the British Institution. He may well have moved to West End from Great Marlborough Street at the suggestion of his neighbour, print seller Josiah Boydell.

Robert Shout (1763-1843) of Treherne House was the sculptor referred to in a Shelley poem describing Leigh Hunt's studio which 'No doubt, Is still adorned with many a cast from Shout.' Shelley was a personal friend. The work of Shout, who was Master of the Masons' Company and an artist-modeller for Wedgwood, is to be found in a number of churches, including Temple Church off Fleet Street.

Father Ignatius Spencer (1799-1864) was one of the Passionist Fathers who lived for a brief while in Poplar House. He was the son of the 2nd Earl Spencer who at the time was First Lord of the Admiralty. Ordained an Anglican minister in 1822, to the dismay of his family, he subsequently converted to Catholicism. In 1847 he became a Passionist Father and later he threatened to visit his sister, Sarah Lady Lyttleton, then a lady-in-waiting to Queen Victoria at Buckingham Palace, while wearing his Passionist habit and sandals. Lady Lyttleton wrote back by return post begging him not to be so foolish as to cause a public stir.

Fr. Spencer was the great, great, great uncle of the late Princess of Wales, Lady Diana Spencer, and the great uncle of Sir Winston Churchill, whom he closely resembled. The Catholic Church is currently considering his canonisation.

The rural nature of Kilburn also attracted a number of artists.

J. C. Ibbetson, (1795-1817), artist.
The wonderfully named Julius Caesar Ibbetson lived in Kilburn from 1787 to 1791 in a house that was roughly opposite the Cock. He was given his unusual name from his uncle Julius and his own caesarean birth in Scarborough. Ibbetson married in 1780 and 'produced off-spring almost as rapidly as pictures'. In 1794, while living in Paddington, his wife died, which brought on an attack of 'brain fever'. When recovered he found that he had been robbed of everything by his servants, but with the help of rich patrons he freed himself from debt and settled in Yorkshire, where he died in 1817. His oil paintings of farm animals were much sought after. He painted the *View of Harrow from Kilburn*, and an engraving of this was used in the first edition of Harrison Ainsworth's *Rookwood*. Ibbetson used rural scenes of Kilburn, (including Kilburn Wells), Hampstead and Hendon in his later paintings, and some of these are in the National Gallery and the Victoria and Albert Museum, while some of his prints are in the British Museum.

John Rathbone (c.1750- 1807), artist.
Born in Cheshire, Rathbone first worked in Manchester before coming to London. He had initially worked in oils but his watercolours, usually landscapes with figures, are more highly thought of. Between 1785 and 1806 he had 48 exhibits at the Royal Academy. Rathbone lived at Kilburn from 1790 to 1795. His close friends were fellow artists, Ibbetson (a neighbour) and George Morland. Morland (1763-1804) did not live in Kilburn but he frequently painted the inns and alehouses of the nearby countryside. The Bell is in the Louvre as *Le Halte*, and the Red Lion appears as *A Door of the Village Inn*.

Oliver Goldsmith (1728-1774), writer.
There is a long cherished tradition that Goldsmith wrote *She Stoops to Conquer* and the *Deserted Village* while lodging in a house in Kilburn in the 1770s. Goldsmith's Place, a small street off the High Road near The Bell and the Red Lion, perpetuated a tradition which seems to have arisen from Boswell's *Life of Johnson* which says that from 1771 to 1774 Goldsmith had taken lodgings at a farmer's house off the Edgware Road. However, this was in Hyde Lane, near the village of Hyde in Hendon. In fact, all the references place Goldsmith at Canons and Hyde and there is no evidence to link him with Kilburn.

The Powell Cotton family owned large amounts of land at the Kilburn end of West End Lane and in Cricklewood, bordering Shoot Up Hill and Edgware Road.

John Powell (1721-1783) purchased the Shoot Up Hill farm and the Liddell farm. He was one of George III's private secretaries and left his money to a nephew, **Arthur Annesley Roberts**, who adopted his uncle's surname. Arthur gained notoriety when he shot and killed Lord Falkland in a duel after it was alleged Falkland had cheated at cards. Arthur was succeeded by his brother **John Powell Roberts Powell**, who made Quex Park in Kent the family home. This explains the many Kentish street names in the area, from Quex and Acol in the South, to Ebbsfleet and Fordwych in the North. John was a keen yachtsman and a campanologist, building a bell tower at Quex Park and installing a peal of twelve bells. He was succeeded by **Henry Perry Cotton** (1806-1881) and a later amalgamation of their surnames gave rise to the more commonly encountered form of 'Powell Cotton.' The estate passed to Henry's son from his first marriage and then to his grandson, **Percy Horace Gordon Powell Cotton** (1866-1940), a great traveller and big game hunter. The stuffed products of his many safaris are on display at Quex Park along with the many photographs he took. Percy spent over fifty years travelling in Africa and the Far East.

LATER RESIDENTS

As the large houses and their grounds fell into the hands of developers, the streets and houses attracted their fair share of interesting inhabitants – artists, actors, eccentrics, entrepreneurs, industrialists, musicians and business men. The balance altered with the passing years or as certain professions fell out of favour, but a blend was maintained. In particular, the proliferation of bed sits and rented flats after the last war offered a large supply of reasonably priced rented accommodation for aspiring actors, artists and writers.

Walter Sickert (1860-1942), artist, 54 Broadhurst Gardens.

In 1885, Sickert married Ellen Cobden, the daughter of the politician, Richard Cobden and moved to Broadhurst Gardens, to a house still being built. Most evenings Sickert would dine out and visit music halls to paint what he saw. The top floor of the house was his studio. When Kate Lawrence, a well known music hall per-

137. Walter Sickert in old age.

former, came to sit for Sickert, she stubbed her toes on the rubble lying around, and let fly with the expletive 'B..... the Bricks!' Ellen and Walter lived in Broadhurst Gardens until 1894. The house was later demolished by the Great Central Railway as part of the works necessary to extend its line into Marylebone.

Alfred Slocombe (d.1899), flower painter, etcher and watercolourist, lived at 2 The Green, West End Lane, in the 1870s and '80s. In 1891 he moved a short distance down the Lane to Cumberland House, one of three large villas built during the 1860s at the West End Lane end of Iverson Road, where he stayed until his death in 1899 after a long illness. His family came from Somerset and in his early years he worked as the chief designer for a firm of silk weavers in Spitalfields, London. He devoted much time and attention to the art of producing a watermark in paper, and exhibited examples of his work at the Great Exhibition of 1862, including portraits of the late Prince Consort and the Prince of Wales.

John Rogers Herbert (1810-1890), artist, The Chimes, West End Lane, near Quex Road.

Born in Essex, Herbert studied at the Royal Academy Schools and made a name for himself as a portrait painter. He was a keen admirer of the architect Augustus Welby Northmore Pugin who was a convert to Catholicism; in fact their friendship so influenced Herbert that he converted too, and his pictures turned increasingly to religious themes. Some of his best known work is in the Houses of Parliament where he was responsible for painting the frescoes in the Peers' Robing Room, which took him eighteen years to complete, using subjects from the Old Testament. Fellow artist Stacy Marks described his colleague.

> 'As he walked or drove slowly along he would discuss art and its professors in a half-humorous, half-oracular manner, rendered piquant by the adoption of a French accent which was characteristic of him in late years.'

John Seymour Lucas (1849-1923) artist, 1 Woodchurch Road.

Lucas was a London 'genre' painter, his canvasses generally depicting scenes set in 17th- and 18th-century costume, or episodes in English History. He also painted portraits including some of other distinguished local residents: Alfred Harmsworth, later Lord Northcliffe, and his friend and neighbour, Banister Fletcher. His wife Marie Elizabeth, (d. 1921) was a portrait and figure painter, who also illustrated children's books, and his daughter likewise became a painter. Both ladies exhibited at the Royal Academy.

A curious architectural feature of Seymour Lucas' house is the Queen Anne doorway which still survives today. When Fairfax House in Putney was demolished, Lucas bought the door with its beautiful shell cupola and installed it in West Hampstead.

Charles Maurice Detmold (1883-1908), artist, who worked in 3 West End Studios, Sherriff Road; and lived and died at 13 Inglewood Road.

Maurice and his twin brother Edward were both artists who produced outstanding bird and animal paintings – their work was used in Kipling's *Jungle Book*. But Maurice's career was cut short by his tragic suicide in 1908. At the time the brothers were living with their uncle in Inglewood Road.

> 'An enquiry was held into the circumstances attending the death of Mr Charles Detmold aged twenty-five. [The] housekeeper said she last saw the deceased at 2.30pm on Thursday, when he asked her not to go to his room, as he had shut some cats in there. The cats were to be chloroformed. Mr Edward Julius Detmold said that when he reached home at seven o'clock ... he went to the bedroom which he and his brother occupied. The door was locked, and so he forced it open. He found the deceased lying on the bed, fully dressed. There was a bag over his head, tied round the neck, and there were three chloroform bottles near. On searching the room witness found two dead cats in a box. They had both been chloroformed.
>
> He had left a suicide note which read; 'This is not the end of a life. I have expressed through my physical means that I am capable of expression, and I am about to lay this aside.' The verdict of the jury was 'suicide whilst of an unsound mind.'

His brother continued to work in watercolours and in etching of birds, animals, insects and landscapes. He exhibited five times at the RA. In 1915 he was living at 7 Priory Court, West Hampstead and by 1929 he had moved to Chelsea. Later he left London and lived in Montgomery in North Wales, where he died 1 July 1957.

Sir Frank Bernard Dicksee, (1853-1928) artist, Greville House, 3 Greville Place

Frank Dicksee came from an artistic family and studied at the Royal Academy Schools. His paintings had a romantic, sentimental or melodramatic theme and for a while he was a fashionable portrait painter, especially popular with female sitters. He was described as 'courteous, warm-hearted and courageous in his convictions'.

He was aged 71 when he was elected 12th President of the Royal Academy in 1924. He died four years later following a serious operation and his funeral service was held at Westminster Abbey.

Sir William Goscombe John, (1860-1952), sculptor RA, 24, 26, 26A Greville Road.

Born in Cardiff, the son of a woodcarver Goscombe John studied in Cardiff, London and Paris. His memorials and bronze statues are to be found all over the world. Nearer to home he did a bronze bust of Sir Frank Dicksee for the Royal Academy in 1907, made the bronze of Sir Arthur Sullivan for St Paul's Cathedral, the statues of Edward VII and Queen Alexandra flanking the main entrance to the Victoria and Albert Museum, and the memorials to the Marquis of Salisbury and the Earl of Cromer in Westminster Abbey. He won the Gold Medal of the Royal Society of British Sculptors in 1942 and exhibited annually at the Academy for 63 years. His work is at the Tate Gallery and the National Museum of Wales. Goscombe John was a courteous and affable man, proud of his Welsh nationality and of his own success.

Louis Wain (1860-1939), artist, 41 Brondesbury Road.

Born in London, Wain studied at the West London School of Art where he was also assistant master. In 1882 he joined the staff of *the Illustrated Sporting and Dramatic News* and four years later that of the *Illustrated London News*. He first began to draw cats in 1883 and this became the principal subject for his art. A rapid worker he could produce 600 drawings a year. His original treatment of cats, which were usually depicted as humans in comical situations, caught the public's imagination and his reputation was established by the 1890s. However, during the First World War he lost popularity and sank into poverty. He lived with his sisters in Brondesbury Road. Largely as a result of financial worry, he developed a mental illness and in 1923 was certified insane. Two years later he was rescued from the pauper ward of an asylum by the aid of a fund raised on his behalf. He transferred to the Bethlem Royal Hospital where he continued to work on his art. He died at Napsbury, near St Albans in 1939. Today his work has become popular again and has recently sold in London auction houses for considerable sums.

Naum Gabo (1890-1977) sculptor, 101 Cholmley Gardens (1939).

Born in Russia, Gabo studied medicine and science in Munich where he made friends with artists such as Kandinski. In 1914 he took up sculpture and then returned to Russia where he established the Constructivist movement with his brother Antonine Pevsner. From 1922 he was in Berlin for ten years where he taught at the Bauhaus. With war approaching he came to England and worked with Ben Nicholson on an international survey of Constructivist art. After the War he moved to the USA and became a professor at Harvard. Gabo is recognised as the leading exponent of the field with his constructions of coloured transparent plastic.

Gilbert Bayes, (1872-1952), sculptor, 4 Greville Place.

London-born Bayes produced the Gold Medals given by the Royal Geographical Society to the explorers Captain Scott and Ernest Shackleton.

David Garsen Bomberg (1890-1957), artist. He lived at several addresses in the area: 10 Fordwych Road (1928-34), then in 1937 he was at 66a Lymington Road, and lastly at 17 Greville Place (1939-40).

A blue plaque commemorates his stay in Fordwych Road which was an important period in his artistic development. Bomberg was one of this country's most important Vorticist and Cubist painters. He was born in Whitechapel and taught by Walter Sickert. Trained at the Slade, he mainly painted still lifes, landscapes and the human head. In *Kilburn Bridges*, he painted the railway bridges at the northern end of Kilburn High Road. Bomberg died in obscurity but his talent has been posthumously recognised.

Joseph Randall-Tussaud (1831-1892), waxwork modeller/artist, Chesterfield House, Iverson Road.

Joseph Randall-Tussaud was the grandson of Madame Tussaud of waxworks fame. When his father died, Joseph became modeller in chief to the Tussaud exhibition. Joseph had money troubles, which might explain why he chose to live at Chesterfield House – its rent was low for its size and it could comfortably accommodate his large family. In 1888 he filed for bankruptcy and died in debt on 5 September 1892, having sold the exhibition to a consortium. By then he had moved from Iverson Road to 62 Broadhurst Gardens.

A modern artist in wool and fabrics – **Kaffe Fassett** – lived in Fordwych Road for several years. Born in San Francisco, Fassett started as a painter.

MUSICIANS

Frederick William Gaisberg (1873-1951), pioneer of the recording industry, 13 Avenue Mansions, Finchley Road and 42 Crediton Hill.

Born in Washington D.C, Gaisberg joined Emile Berliner at the Gramophone Company in 1894. He was sent to London four years later to take charge of its newly opened recording studio in Maiden Lane near the Strand. He made many recordings of music hall artists such as Dan Leno, Marie Lloyd and Vesta Tilley, and later famous singers such as Melba, Patti, Tetrazzini, Chaliapin and Gigli. But perhaps it was the quality of his 1902 Caruso recordings that laid the foundations for the modern recording industry, as until then the gramophone had not been taken seriously. Gaisberg stayed with the company until he retired in 1939, remaining a keen judge of musical talent. He snapped up the young conductor John Barbirolli in 1927 after he had stepped in at short notice to replace Sir Thomas Beecham, and he also helped to launch the career of Yehudi Menuhin. He was instrumental in encouraging his friend Sir Edward Elgar to write his Third Symphony (only recently and controversially completed) and Elgar dedicated his last work *Mina* to Gaisberg.

Max Jaffa, band leader lived for about two years at 5 Hillcrest Court. More recently, **Tony Hooper,** one of the founders of the group The Strawberry Hill Boys later renamed The Strawbs lived in the basement of 32 Dennington Park Road. Singer **Olivia Newton John** purchased one of the first flat conversions in the road, the penthouse of no. 9. Nearby, in Inglewood Road, singer **Jimmy Sommerville** (Bronski Beat / The Communards) occupied 12a. In the fifties, 27 Crediton Hill was home to **Edric O'Connor** a talented Trinidadian singer while **Errol Brown** of the group Hot Chocolate lived in Hillfield Road. Jazz musician and club owner **Ronnie Scott** was living in Messina Avenue in 1981 when he received an OBE.

Dusty Springfield (1939-1999) singer.
Dusty was born as Mary O'Brien at the Caerthillian Maternity Home, 87 Fordwych Road. Her family home was in Sumatra Road. With her brother Tom, she formed a group called The Springfields in 1960, from which she took her name. When they disbanded in 1963, she went solo and her career blossomed, but after 1968 personal problems took their toll and her performances ceased for several years. However, she made a comeback just before her recent death. She is seen by many people to have been the best female rock singer that Britain has produced.

ENTREPRENEURS

Probably the most famous local entrepreneur is **Alfred Harmsworth** (1865-1922) later **Viscount Northcliffe**, the newspaper proprietor. He and his family lived at several addresses in the neighbourhood, including 94 Boundary Road, 77 Iverson Road, 37 Sherriff Road (since renumbered as 53) as well 31 Pandora Road, where he is commemorated by a Blue Plaque, even though his stay there was brief (1888-1891).

His wife to be, Mary Milner, lived with her parents at 98 West End Lane. They were married in 1888 when he was earning around £200 a year and he had to borrow the cash to buy an engagement ring. Their first home was in Pandora Road where the rent was £26 a year.

Harmsworth realised there was an enormous untapped market for popular newspapers and he went on to found both the *Daily Mail* and *Daily Mirror*, as well as several magazines. His business premises in Paternoster Square (four miles distant) were within walking distance of Pandora Road. Apparently Harmsworth disliked both the house and the area, although he later admitted his time there was a happy one. Once successful he left West Hampstead for Broadstairs. The road name was immortalised by his Pandora Publishing Company.

138. Alfred Harmsworth, cartoon by Spy in 1895

William Friese-Greene (1855-1921), pioneer of cinema, 136 Maida Vale.

Friese-Greene was as important to moving pictures as Harmsworth was to popular publishing, but far less successful. And despite the fact that he was also commemorated by one of the district's few blue plaques, Camden Council recently gave permission for his old house to be demolished. Born in Bristol in 1855, Friese-Greene was apprenticed to a photographer, later moving to Bath where he opened a studio of his own. He grew increasingly unhappy with 'frozen' pictures and came to London in 1885 where he began experimenting. His work finally culminated in a roll of celluloid film, some fifty feet long. The first moving pictures were taken in Hyde Park one Sunday morning in 1889 and he took out his master patent for cinematography, two years before Edison's Kinetoscope in 1891. He died in 1921 and is buried in Highgate Cemetery.

Albert Eustace Short (1875-1932) and **Horace Leonard Short** (1872 -1917), aircraft designers 1, Ranulf Road.

The three Short brothers, Horace, Albert and Oswald, are famous for their pioneering work in airship and aircraft design. Horace survived childhood meningitis, apparently complicated by hydrocephalus which left him with an enlarged skull. In 1890 Horace decided to visit his uncle in Australia. En route he met Robert Louis Stevenson in Samoa; was next captured by cannibals but was spared the pot when they decided to make him their king, perhaps because of his unusual appearance. He escaped and ended up as manager of a silver mine in Mexico. Following their father's death in 1893 which left the family almost penniless, Albert was sent to bring Horace home, but instead, Horace gave him £500 and sent him back to England, following on a year or so later. In 1908 the three men joined forces as Short Brothers, Aeronautical Engineers to design and manufacture aeroplanes which included six aircraft for Orville and Wilbur Wright.

The outbreak of the First World War brought about an increase in production which by then included bombers and airships – Horace is credited with inventing the name 'blimp', and also a folding wing seaplane which was used in the war. He died in 1917 but the company continued to grow steadily, diversifying to build boats and lightweight bodies for London buses. Albert died in Maidstone in 1932. He had a heart attack while at the wheel of his sea plane although he managed to land it safely.

Thomas Bate (d. 1913), local tradesman, estate agent and property speculator.

Originally from Devon, in 1861 he was living at 246 Belsize Road, where he gave his profession as that of tea dealer. By 1881 he and his large family had moved to 54 High Road. Bate was elected as a Hampstead vestryman in the 1860s until his resignation in 1884. He speculated in property speculation in the Belsize Road area, where he built Kilburn 'Town Hall' (*see p.86*) and sold the site of the old Kilburn Well. He moved on to develop roads on the Powell Cotton estate between West End Lane and Priory Road (Cleve, Acol and Woodchurch). He sold the building which later became West Hampstead 'Town Hall' in Broadhurst Gardens. He also acted as local agent to the Royal Agricultural Society and was thanked for his 'efficient services' during the

1879 Show at Queen's Park. Though he went bankrupt in 1895 his estate agent's business survived. Bate died in 1907 at 33 Brondesbury Road.

Ernest Owers (d.1938) estate agent and local developer. Office West End Lane, home 288 Finchley Road.

Owers trained as a solicitor's clerk, later working in the Stock Exchange before joining his father's estate agent firm. In 1879 he started his own office adjoining the newly-opened West Hampstead Underground station. To begin with he would walk home each night to Shepherds Bush, but soon moved in over the shop. Locals remember how Owers 'used to dash about, driving a fast horse, a large cigar always in the corner of his mouth, with prospective purchasers of land', so it is not surprising he bought one of the first cars in the neighbourhood. Owers was involved in many of the land deals and developments in both West Hampstead and Golders Green where he set up a land sales office before the Northern line opened, working from a hut.

Robert Allen Yerbury (d. 1894), major builder, St Margaret's Lodge, Kilburn High Road.

Yerbury was a Somerset man. He was already a successful builder when he moved to Kilburn, describing himself in the 1861 census as employing 36 men and boys. Yerbury's firm rapidly expanded and landed the contracts for many important municipal buildings. Locally, it built Hampstead's first Electricity Supply Station in Lithos Road, the Gordon Memorial Schools in Cambridge Road and renovated St Paul's Church, Kilburn Square. Yerbury was also instrumental in setting up what later became the Abbey Road Building Society.

> 'Mr Alfred Pope, who was one of the earliest Directors of the Abbey Road Building Society told me that in the seventies he and other workmen were in the employ of a Mr Yerbury, a builder of Kilburn. They were all members of the Abbey Road Church Benefit Building Society, and he suggested that they should form, in connection with the Benefit Society, a building society with the idea of saving sufficient to purchase houses for themselves. The benefit Society had a membership of over 500. The proposal met with a ready response. A large number joined, payments being made weekly. These, then, were the founders of the Abbey Road Society.'

139. John Spedan Lewis, c.1904.

Although he was generally successful, at one point Yerbury went to the bankruptcy court with liabilities of £16,500 and assets of only £12,000.

John Spedan Lewis (1885-1963), of John Lewis Stores, North Hall, Mortimer Crescent

John Spedan Lewis, son of John Lewis who had founded the Oxford Street store, was responsible for the foundation of the John Lewis Partnership which still today, despite recent proposals, administers the stores around the country. Spedan Lewis was firmly committed to the idea of profit-sharing amongst his employees and to the restriction of profits distributed to shareholders. He later lived at Spedan Tower, a house set in extensive grounds on West Heath Road. Spedan Lewis was a keen naturalist: a visitor described the house in Kilburn:

> 'We used to play tennis with him at North Hall in Hampstead before we were married and we'd have some very keen tennis matches. He had a tennis court made with cages at each end in which he kept lynxes. One of these cages was up against the back netting so if you went to pick up your ball, there was a lynx about

a foot away. It was quite extraordinary but that was typical of him - he loved wild animals.'

Mr Lewis also offered visits to his staff members:

'I have here a small collection of birds which are, for the most part, rather exceptionally interesting. To see them properly takes about three-quarters of an hour or a little more. If any Partners would like to see them and will write to Mrs Lewis' Private Secretary, arrangements will be made with my bird-keeper and a card of invitation will be sent for a particular time with directions how to find the house. '

WRITERS AND THESPIANS

Authors of all types outnumber theatricals and musicians.

Douglas Jerrold (1803-1857) , playwright and editor of *Punch*. Died at Kilburn Priory.

The son of an actor, he taught himself numerous languages and immersed himself in literature. After a period in the Navy, Jerrold began to write for a number of magazines. He also wrote successful plays: for example, *Black-eyed Susan* ran for four hundred performances in 1829. When *Punch* began in 1841, Jerrold was a constant contributor right up to his death. In 1856

141. *Annie Besant.*

140. *Douglas Jerrold.*

he moved from St John's Wood to Kilburn Priory where he died in 1857. After his death, Charles Dickens organised performances which raised £2,000 for his family.

Annie Besant (1847-1933), political author and social reformer, 'Oaklands', 12 Mortimer Road (later Crescent).

Born in London as Annie Wood, she married the Reverend Frank Besant when she was twenty years old. They had two children, and during her daughter's serious illness with whooping cough, Annie suffered a crisis of faith and never regained her religious belief. In 1873 the couple separated and Annie became interested in the ideas of the National Secular Society, whose leading light was Charles Bradlaugh. Annie had discovered a kindred spirit. She apparently moved to Kilburn to be near Bradlaugh who lived down the road in St John's Wood. Annie began to work as a committed freethinker, an atheist at a time when it was not popular in polite society. She joined the Fabian Society and in1888 organised a famous strike of matchmaking girls at Bryant & May, and formed their union. Then she announced her conversion to Theosophy as taught by Madame Blavatsky. She became the head of the Theosophical Society and was elected as president in 1907. From 1895 onwards Annie Besant worked in India where she knew Gandhi and was involved in the growth of nationalism.

Thomas Hardy (1840-1928), author, rented lodgings on Edgware Road between April 1862 and May 1863, when he came to London to study architecture under Arthur Blomfield. Hardy lived first at no. 3 and then briefly no. 9 Clarence Place, a terrace of small houses roughly opposite the present State Cinema. Hardy worshipped in St Mary's, Abbey Road, which he described as 'rather to my taste' but he never used Kilburn as an inspiration for any of his novels. He left Clarence Place for Westbourne Park Villas.

Alan Alexander Milne (1882-1956), better known as A.A. Milne, the author of the *Winnie the Pooh* stories, Henley House, Mortimer Crescent

In 1878 John Vine Milne took over Henley House School at the corner of Kilburn Priory, where his son was born four years later. Milne records that his father paid one hundred pounds for the goodwill which consisted of:

> 'Twenty or thirty desks and half-a-dozen inky boys whose parents had been too lazy to find a better school for them. Henley House was one of those private schools, then so common, now so unusual, for boys of all ages. Of the fifty boys, perhaps fifteen were boarders.'

Matters at Henley House improved slightly under his father's management although the school was never a financial success. It later provided employment for H.G. Wells as well as a place to study for the young Alfred Harmsworth.

H.G. Wells (1866-1946), author, Henley House, Mortimer Crescent.

Wells was the first science teacher ever appointed at Henley House in 1888. He stayed for a year, walking to Kilburn from his lodgings in Fitzroy Road, off Primrose Hill. He found the equipment 'skimpy' and was given just one sovereign by J.V. Milne to buy equipment. He found a cupboard full of broken flasks, carefully arranged by his predecessor who had broken them all in the course of a single lesson, trying to produce oxygen by heating potassium permanganate; the glass was just not strong enough to withstand irregular heating over a Bunsen burner. One of Wells' pupils told him it had been 'a very great lesson indeed!' Wells suggested dissecting a rabbit, and Milne gave his cautious approval, so long as it would not be 'indelicate' – one never knows what parents will find to object to.

142. H.G. Wells.

Olive Schreiner (1855-1920), novelist and feminist, Mutrix Road

South African born Olive Schreiner lived in England between 1881 and 1889. She came to study medicine but was prevented from continuing her studies by ill health. Her novel *The Story of an African Farm* was published in 1881 and proved a great success. She went on a number of retreats to counteract the toll her popularity took on both her physical and mental health. In 1886 she stayed for a month at St Dominic's Convent in Mutrix Road before moving to Harrow. She wrote to a friend:

> I'm not allowed out after nine at night: the house is locked and the nuns go to bed then. It isn't like London this quiet house with the nuns in their white and black dresses walking so silently about.

143. Israel Zangwill.

Israel Zangwill (1864-1926), author and a founder of Zionism

Zangwill lived at 24 Oxford Road from 1893 to 1899. As a writer his best known works were *King of the Schnorrers* and *Children of the Ghetto*. In 1895 he met Theodor Herzl there and they discussed the notion of Zionism. Deeply impressed, Zangwill helped Herzl in his first address to a London audience at the Maccabean Club.

John Drinkwater (1882-1937) playwright and poet, North Hall, Mortimer Place/Crescent

Drinkwater lived here from 1934 until his death in 1937. He wrote a large number of poems and plays between 1908 and 1937. Like his father he worked in the theatre and he co-founded the Pilgrim Players which became the Birmingham Repertory Theatre. He both acted and wrote, establishing his writing career with a play about Abraham Lincoln which transferred to the Lyric Theatre at Hammersmith.

Lady Sara Louisa Blomfield (d. 1939), author, 8 Burgess Hill.

Sara was the second wife of Sir Arthur William Blomfield, the well known architect. She helped to popularise the Bahian faith which was founded in Persia during the 19th century. Abdu'l-Baha, the son of the founder, visited England in 1911 and again in 1913 and stayed with Lady Blomfield. She wrote articles about the Bahian faith and travelled around Europe to spread the word to a wider audience.

She also supported Mrs Pankhurst and the Suffragette movement. After the First World War she made friends with Miss Eglantyne Jebb and was involved in establishing the Save the Children Fund in 1920. Until her death at the end of 1939 she devoted herself to Bahianism and published several books and articles on the subject.

George Orwell (1903-1950), author, 10A Mortimer Crescent.

George Orwell, whose real name was Eric Blair, moved to Kilburn from nearby Abbey Road in 1942, renting the lower half of the house. 10A Mortimer Crescent, which no longer exists, apparently delighted Orwell at the time:

> '[It] conjured up those middle-to-lower-middle-class households on which his mind loved to dwell. "They would probably have kept a Buttons here," he said, enchanted at the thought. The sitting-room with a background of furniture dating from more prosperous generations of bygone Blairs, two or three 18th century family portraits hanging on the walls, might well have been the owner's study in a country house.'

However not everyone saw the Mortimer Crescent flat in the same light as Orwell. Comments about a 'remarkably dreary, icily cold, damp basement' were made by his friends. Apparently the boiler would go out if someone didn't get up in the night to stoke it! Unfit for active war service, Orwell was working for the foreign service of the BBC, moving on to become literary editor of the Socialist magazine, *Tribune*. He and his wife moved to Islington in 1944.

Evelyn Waugh (1903-1966) and his brother **Alec Waugh** (1898-1981), authors, 11 Hillfield Road.

Arthur and Catherine Waugh moved to Hillfield Road in 1895 from rooms over a dairy on nearby Finchley Road.

Evelyn Arthur St John Waugh was born in this house on 28 October 1903. His parents were well pleased with their baby, although Arthur had been hoping for a girl. The enthusiasm of his elder brother, Alec, was short-lived. A boisterously athletic infant, Alec had converted the nursery, until then entirely his domain, into a cricket pitch where he played a complicated game of his own invention. By bouncing a tennis ball from the wall he could bat to his own bowling. He judged himself 'out' when the ball landed on the net which protected his new brother.

Edmund Clerihew Bentley (1875-1956), Journalist.

Bentley lived at 28 Lymington Road during the 1920s. He met G.K. Chesterton when they both attended St Paul's school and they remained lifelong friends. While sitting in a science class, Bentley came up with the following lines:

Sir Humphrey Davy
Abominated gravy.
He lived in the odium
Of having discovered Sodium.

This was the beginning of what Chesterton called 'the severe and stately form of free verse known as the Clerihew'. Davy was joined by others and the results were published in 1905 as *Biography for Beginners*. Like many people, Bentley was fascinated by Conan Doyle's Sherlock Holmes stories, but he was irritated by the detective's infallibility. He decided to write a different kind of story in which the detective's convincing solution was wrong. *Trent's Last Case* was published in 1913 and became a best seller. It was even described as the best detective novel of the century.

Sir Israel Gollancz, (1864-1930) lived at 'Melrose' no.15 Shoot Up Hill, (now demolished, it stood a few hundred yards north of Exeter Road). His brother and sister lived almost opposite at 38. Sir Israel was a writer and a professor of English Language and Literature at King's College London. He was also a founder member of the British Academy. Victor Gollancz, the publisher, was his nephew.

John 'White Fox' Hargrave (1894-1982), artist and writer, Fortune Green Road.

In a working life of seventy years John Gordon Hargrave was an artist, illustrator, cartoonist, copywriter, Boy Scout commissioner, inventor, author, and psychic healer. He published a regular series of articles and pamphlets about the values of scouting and open-air life under the name of 'White Fox'. His wartime experiences convinced him that civilisation had failed, and a programme of outdoor education was needed for regeneration. He found that his views were not accepted by Baden-Powell and he was promptly expelled from the Scouts. To put his ideas into action he founded the 'Kibbo Kift' in 1920 to train a body of men and women who would act as a catalyst on 'a corrupt and directionless society' and lead it back to health. The name 'Kibbo Kift' was taken from an old Kentish dialect phrase meaning 'a proof of great strength'.

His followers adopted the uniform of a green shirt. Direct action was taken and green painted bricks were thrown through the windows of Downing Street. The Green Shirts found themselves attacked by the media and by both communists and the fascists. Although few in number, they became quite well known and the Advisory Committee included Havelock Ellis, H.G. Wells and Julian Huxley, while other KK supporters included Compton Mackenzie and Augustus John. After the war Hargrave tried to revive Kibbo Kift but the movement met with little success and in 1951 it was agreed to dissolve the party.

Meantime Hargrave had written several best selling novels; *Summer Time Ends* (1935) received praise from Ezra Pound and John Steinbeck, but Cyril Connolly said, 'I found this literally unreadable'. In 1937 he had also invented a 'moving map' automatic navigation system for aircraft and thirty years later, he discovered that a version had been installed in Concorde. Despite a nine-year legal battle, Hargrave failed to get any financial settlement. It was a crushing disappointment from which he never fully recovered. He was however heartened by the staging of a rock musical about the Kibbo Kift performed at the 1976 Edinburgh Festival and at the Crucible Theatre, Sheffield the following year.

Doris Lessing, author, currently lives off Mill Lane. Her first home in the neighbourhood was nearby, at 11 Kingscroft Road. She spent her childhood in Zimbabwe before coming to London in 1949. The following year her first novel *The Grass Is Singing* became a best seller. She has written numerous novels and several volumes of her autobiography have been published.

Sean Connery, actor.
In the 1950s Connery, an up-and-coming but still struggling actor, rented a one-room flat in Brondesbury Villas. He later bought 3 Wavel Mews, three rooms above a garage, which he renovated himself. He is listed in a 1959 directory under his own name of T. (Tammy) Connery.

The late **Sir Dirk Bogarde,** actor and writer, lived at number 39 St George's Road, now renamed Priory Terrace, before moving to 173 Goldhurst Terrace. His parents came to live in Kilburn in 1920 after their honeymoon and, to begin with, let out rooms to artist and writer friends. The family appears to have moved house shortly after he was born about 1923. His father Ulric van den Bogaerde, was art editor of *The Times*.

The famous comedy double act of Tony Hancock and Sid James both lived in the neighbourhood. **Tony Hancock** lived for a short while at 6 Harvard Court in Honeybourne Road which was the home of his wife, Freddie Ross and her parents. He later made *The Rebel* a film about an unsuccessful artist, for which houses in Dennington Park Road were hired for some of the location shots, though the footage was never used. **Sidney James,** comedian, was at 21 Lymington Road from 1954-6.

This has since been demolished and replaced by a small block of flats. Sid's bar – which occupied a complete room of his flat – consisted of plain white-wood furniture and wall-to-wall deep scarlet carpet. The walls were covered in just two kinds of decoration – a cluster of framed photographs of Sid in his film and stage roles, and scores of miniature liquor bottles. The shelves, as Sid informed any new guest, he had built himself. James moved on to a much larger house in Gunnersbury Avenue, Ealing.

George Layton (actor, writer, director) lived at 28 and 34 Dennington Park Road during the 1970s, later moving to the 'Greek Roads' near Fortune Green. **Michael Elphick** (actor) lived at 37.

Joan Collins actress, and **Jackie Collins,** actress and writer. 20 Hillcrest Court, Shoot Up Hill.

Their parents Joe and Elsa were probably the first occupants of the flat in 1936. Joe was a theatrical and vaudeville agent, who went into partnership with Lew Grade. He described baby Joan as 'just a dark little nothing, a scruffy little child with a few tufts of hair. Very ordinary'. Jackie was born round the corner from their new home in a nursing home in Fordwych Road, the Caerthillian Maternity Home. The family soon moved to Alexandra Court, Maida Vale.

Crediton Hill was home to **Eric Thompson**, author of the English version of the children's series *The Magic Roundabout*. His wife ,the actress **Phyllida Law,** and his Oscar-winning daughter, **Emma Thompson,** still live in the neighbourhood as does **Bert Kwok**, perhaps best known for playing the deadpan servant to Peter Sellers' zany policeman in the Inspector Clouseau films. **Imelda Staunton**, **Emily Richard** and her husband **Edward Petherbridge** are also locals.

Tom Conti, actor, lived in Exeter Road during the 1970s, and from 1978 to 1984 at 10 Mowbray Road.

Richard Wilson, perhaps best known for his portrayal of the grumpy Victor Meldrew in the TV series *One Foot In The Grave*, lived in a bedsitter in 25 Lyncroft Gardens from 1959 to 1965. When he moved in Richard was trying to get acting jobs but working as a travelling salesman.

> 'Up two flights, on the side of the house, it was a dark room, with a single bed in one corner, and a wash basin in the other, a gas fire with a chair on either side, a Baby Belling gas ring for boiling a kettle, and a gas meter which had constantly to be fed with coins or so it seemed. The bathroom and toilet along the corridor were shared with other tenants in the house, as was the pay telephone.'

Each day Richard travelled to work on the number 28 bus.

Lilli Palmer (1914-1986), actress moved into 17 Parsifal Road in the late 1930s, which she shared with her mother and two sisters.

> The rent was cheap, and it had plenty of bedrooms and a tiny back garden. From the start we referred to it as the second-ugliest house in London, allowing for the possibility that there might be an even uglier one.

Not really a fair description while the garden, by London standards, is huge!

After training as an actress in Berlin, Lilli came to England in 1933 and had a few small parts before she appeared in Hitchcock's film *Secret Agent* (1936) with John Gielgud and Peter Lorre. She was married to her co-star Rex Harrison from 1943 to 1957 and for much of the time they lived and worked in Hollywood and Broadway. Her second marriage to the Argentine actor and writer, Carlos Thompson, lasted over twenty years. In a long career Lilli appeared on stage and in over 70 films.

Another famous actor spent part of his pre-war childhood in Hillfield Road. **Joss Ackland** (b. 1928) moved to no. 86 when he was three, and then onto Fordwych Road in 1938.

OTHER NOTABLES

Arthur Munby (1828-1910), poet, author and **Hannah Cullwick (1833-1909)**

Hannah was born in Shropshire, and spent her working life as a servant, starting when she was just eight years old. In 1854 she met Arthur Munby, a poet who worked in the Ecclesiastical Commissioners' office. In August 1856 she went to work as a servant for a newly married couple, the Jacksons, who lived at 22 Carlton Villas, Kilburn. In March 1861 Jackson's debts forced the couple to leave the neighbourhood. Hannah got a new job with the neighbours, the Fosters, where she remained until March 1864. Sometimes Munby visited her while she was working at Carlton Villas, or they met in the streets nearby. Munby had an obsession with working-class women – one biography described him as a 'man of two worlds'. They adopted a 'master' and 'servant' relationship, with Hannah calling him 'Massa'. Although they lived apart for much of the time, they had a secret eighteen-year relationship before marrying in 1873. Hannah remained in a servant position living in the basement kitchen of Munby's chambers. After four years she returned to Shropshire, later moving into a cottage Munby rented for her at Hadley.

Granny Dripping Pot

Granny Dripping was a crossing sweeper, one of a vast army of men, women and children who swept the road in front of pedestrians, cleaning away mud and manure that might otherwise cling to their long dresses or spatter their trousers. Her post was at the end of the steps over the Underground railway lines, where Priory Road met Broadhurst Gardens. She was recalled by a local resident, a small boy at the turn of the century as 'shrivelled up and poorly clad'. The steps may have been more used then than now but as he observed:

> It is doubtful whether she removed more than a pound or two of dust or mud in the course of a month. 'Granny Dripping Pot' was sorely baited by the children of the district, at whom she would fiercely brandish her besom looking for all the world like the witch in Hansel and Gretel.

Her name probably owed more to a habit of eating bread and dripping sandwiches, rather than a lack of a handkerchief. In the 1950s and 60s the steps from Broadhurst Gardens to the bridge over the railway line were known locally as Granny's Stairs.

William Tegetmeier (1816-1912), naturalist, 19 Westbere Road.

Tegetmeier, who worked with Darwin, studied breeding and variation in animals. He proved the homing faculty of pigeons by flights from Crystal Palace to Brussels, and he looked at 'the destructive influence of the sparrow'.

The self styled **Baron Corvo** (1860-1913), whose real name was Frederick William Rolfe, lived in lodgings in Iverson Road in 1886, and then from 1899-1904 at 69 Broadhurst Gardens (since demolished). Rolfe heard of the vacancy through a friend who lived in the house and is supposed to have immortalised the tiny room in his book *Hadrian the VII.*

> 'The attic was eleven feet square, low pitched and with half the ceiling slanting to four foot from the floor... The armchair was placed directly in front of the fireplace, the ordinary garret-coloured iron fireplace and mantel of a suburban lodging-house attic. The door was at a yard to the fireplace, at a right-angle.'

Born in Cheapside, the son of a piano maker, Rolfe worked as a teacher in London, Essex, Hampshire and Cambridge. Received into the Catholic Church in 1886 he began to call himself the Reverend Father Rolfe. Then followed various appointments in schools and colleges from which Rolfe was dismissed after short periods. While in debt in Rome he was supported by a Duchess who gave him the title of Baron Corvo. He returned to England and, using his fake title, he attempted to make his way in society, but with no success. He began to write, and his first book was published in 1898. His most enduring novel *Hadrian the VII* (1904), was written while he lived in West Hampstead. Four years later he left for Venice where he lived a degenerate life that ended in his death in 1913.

Banister Fletcher (1833-1899), and his sons: **Sir Banister Flight Fletcher** (1866-1953) and **Herbert Phillips Fletcher** (1872-1917), were all architects. The family lived at Anglebay, 21 Woodchurch Road.

Both Banister and his eldest son Banister Flight were successful architects who together produced *A History of Architecture on the Comparative Method* (1896), still considered a vital reference work. Anglebay (now demolished) on the corner of Woodchurch Road and West End Lane, may have been to Banister's own design. He designed several other distinctive houses in nearby roads, for example 82 Compayne Gardens and 5 Cleve Road. Banister Flight was called to the Bar in 1908 and knighted in 1919. Locally, he designed the International College at the corner of Lymington Road and Finchley Road.

Herbert Fletcher became a partner in the family firm of architects. When war broke out he joined the Royal Flying Corps and from March 1915 to February 1916 he was lent to the French Navy as senior military observer for reconnaissance work in seaplanes from Aden to Gallipoli. For this work he was awarded the Croix de Guerre three times, and he also won the DSO.

Professor Silvanus Thompson, physicist, 'Morland', 88 Chislett Road, renamed Compayne Gardens in 1936

Born in York in 1851, Thompson held many prestigious positions during his lifetime including that of Professor of Experimental Physics at Bristol and Physics Professor in the City and Guilds Technical College, Finsbury. His obituary described him as 'an all round physicist with a special affection for optics'. He wrote several textbooks and was also 'known to deliver a good lecture'.

144. J.L. Garvin.

James Louis Garvin (1868-1947) Editor of *The Observer*, 9 Greville Place.

Garvin wrote on 'world issues' for the *Daily Telegraph* and was editor in chief of the *Encyclopaedia Britannica* in 1926. He was editor of *The Observer* from 1908 to 1942.

Charles Douglas-Home (1937-1986) Editor of *The Times*, 18 Mortimer Crescent.
After Army work in Kenya he was the military correspondent for the *Daily Express*. In 1964 he joined *The Times* as the political correspondent and then worked his way up to become editor in 1982.

Philip Arthur Layman, herbalist, beekeeper and distiller lived at 7 Pandora Road.

He was a very large man with a very timid wife. In 1934 he was fined for 'possessing an illicit still and depositing spirits at his address with intent to defraud his Majesty of duty'. The still comprised banana skins in an old oil can and was described by the Magistrate as 'a foul and filthy mixture .... a lethal type of cocktail'. In the 1950s he was a familiar sight, riding in a stately, upright manner round the local streets on his bicycle, sometimes in pursuit of an escaped swarm of bees. The rear ground floor rooms of his house were gloomy and dark due to a jungle of foliage in the garden which obscured light from the windows. An early believer in ecology and alternative medicine, he planted many shrubs to encourage butterflies and sold herbal remedies.

Compton Collier, photographer, 103 West End Lane.

Cecil Beaton talks about Compton Collier in his autobiography when she took pictures of him and his mother with their dog. He describes her as:

> An agile spinster of over seventy with a pale brown face of minor distinctiveness. She projected a personality that brooked no nonsense, and no interruption. Behind the camera her performance was dynamic – even acrobatic. In order to stimulate the interest of her subjects she would jump up and down, wave an arm, squeak a rubber dog, and hum in a high musical voice.

She was a very sound sleeper. During an air raid in the last war 'when the roof was blown off the house and all her rooms but two were destroyed [she] went on snoring'. This was probably the raid in June 1944 that damaged much of the opposite side of the Lane, between Acol and Woodchurch Roads.

Kim Philby, spy, 18 Acol Road.

Kim Philby is probably the most notorious resident of this district. His father, the extravagantly named Harry St John Bridger Philby, was an explorer who succeeded T.E. Lawrence as the British representative in Transjordan. Kim Philby hit the national headlines when he was exposed as a Russian spy. He had warned fellow spies Burgess and Maclean in 1951, but after their escape suspicion fell on Philby. He finally fled to Russia in 1963 where he settled in Moscow and reached the rank of Colonel in the KGB. Philby died in 1988 and was buried with full Russian military honours.

Joseph Rotblat, physicist and peace campaigner, currently lives off Mill Lane.

Born in 1908 and educated in Poland he began his work in atomic physics in his home country. From 1939 he worked at the University of Liverpool. Rotblat worked at the US Los Alamos Centre during the last war, developing the atom bomb, but resigned once it became apparent Germany could not produce a bomb of its own. The devastation produced by dropping the atom bomb on Japan caused him to devote his life to the prevention of nuclear warfare. He is president of 'Pugwash', the worldwide movement for peace, and in 1995 he was awarded the Nobel Peace Prize. He is also a Freeman of the London Borough of Camden.

Sir Learie Constantine, cricketer, 11 Kendal Court, Shoot Up Hill

Born in Trinidad in 1901, Sir Learie became a famous international cricketer. He subsequently became a lawyer and held numerous official posts such as the High Commissioner for Trinidad and Tobago in London, and a Governor of the BBC. He was given a life peerage in 1969 and he died in 1971.

West Hampstead was home to not one but two, chess grandmasters, **Nigel Short**, in Hemstal Road, and **Jonathan Speelman**.

Martin Bell lived at 7 Ambassador Court, Holmdale Road for a while. A news reporter more recently known as 'the man in the white suit,' Bell was elected an Independent MP in 1997.

Ken Livingstone, MP, leader of the GLC and local councillor.

'Red Ken' as he was dubbed during the Thatcher era, has lived at several addresses in the neighbourhood: Lymington Road, Gascony Avenue and 26 Kingsgate Road (1983-1989).

Pevsner in his *Buildings of England* volume on north London declared that, 'West Hampstead need be visited by only those in search of Victorian churches'. We hope that this illustrated history of Kilburn and West Hampstead has demonstrated that there is a great deal more of interest in this cosmopolitan area than ecclesiastical architecture.

Further Reading

The following were the main sources of reference used:

Ackland, Joss, *I must be in there somewhere* (1989)
Alpert, Michael, 'West Hampstead's Railway Invasion,' *Camden History Review* 7 (1979).
Apple, Raymond, *The History of Hampstead Synagogue 1892-1967* (1967).
Aston, Mark, *The Cinemas of Camden* (1997).
Baines, Frederick E., *Records of the Manor, Parish and Borough of Hampstead* (1890).
Barratt, Thomas J., *The Annals of Hampstead* (3 Vols) (1912).
Cross, G., *Suffolk Punch* (1939).
Dictionary of National Biography CD-Rom (1995).
Hampstead at War (reptd by the Camden History Society).
Jennings, Trevor, *The School in Mill Lane* (1963).
Landstone, C., *I Gatecrashed* (1976).
Park. John J., *The Topography and Natural History of Hampstead* (1814).
Pocock, Tom (ed.), *Travels of a London Schoolboy 1826-1830* (rev. edn 1996).
Redley, M., 'The End of the Cock and Hoop', *Camden History Review 9 (1981).*
Snow, Len, *Willesden Past* (1994).
Snow, Len, *Brent – A Pictorial History* (1990).
Thompson, F. M. L., *Hampstead – The Building of a Borough 1650-1964* (1974).
Tucker, J., *Emmanuel Church* (1981).
The Victoria County History, Middlesex Volume 7 (1982).
The Victoria County History, Middlesex Volume 9 (1989).
Wade, Christopher (ed), *The Streets of West Hampstead* (1992).
Weindling, Dick, 'The Fight for Fortune Green', *Camden History Review* 10 (1982).
Weindling, Dick, 'West End House and The Beckford Scandal', *Camden History Review* 20 (1996).
Who's Who CD-Rom (1996).
Woollett, Caroline, *A Child's Eye View of West Hampstead* (1995).

INDEX

An asterisk indicates an illustration or caption